Dater's Ed

The Instruction Manual for Parents

Lisa Jander

"mama j"

First Published by Manna Enterprises in the USA
Lake Orion, Michigan

June 2008

— Dater's Ed —
The Instruction Manual for Parents

All text in **bold italics** is used with permission
from the Michigan Department of State.
All verbatim quotes were taken directly from either
the *"Road Test Study Guide"* publication or
"What Every Driver Must Know" (WEDMK) publication.

Thank you to the Michigan Department of State.
For information about Dater's Ed Please visit our website at
www.DatersEd.com

Edited by: Erin Waugh
Cover designed by: Christos Schizas

Library of Congress Cataloging-in-Publication Data

Jander, Lisa,
Dater's Ed : The Instruction Manual for Parents / Lisa Jander

ISBN: 978-0-615-21578-5
Parenting/Teen/Dating/Relationships/Adolescence

2008930482

Copyright Registered: 2008
First Published by Manna Enterprises in the USA
Lake Orion, MI

June 2008

About the Author

Lisa Jander is a Certified Life Coach, public speaker, and former director of a dating service in California. As the mother of two teens and surrogate to hundreds more, 'Mama J' shares her unique relationship insights with her readers in this, her first book, *Dater's Ed*. She and her husband Owen live in Lake Orion, Michigan. Oops, with their children.

Lisa is a 14-year-old trapped in an old person's body. She plays a cello named Sophia, wields a mean sledgehammer, and has more friends than dirty dishes. After a profound midlife awakening, Lisa decided to wrestle her dream to the floor and make it behave.

Lisa doesn't know anything about cars, including her own.

She can be contacted at Lisa@DatersEd.com. If you don't have any luck finding her there, she is probably on her roof watching hot air balloons with a bunch of crazy teens singing off key. If you see Lisa wandering aimlessly in a mall parking lot with her keys in her hand, please help her find her car.

About the Editor

Erin Waugh, Lisa's merciless editor, phantom writer, and word masseuse, is also the mother of a teen in Lake Orion, Michigan, "Where Living is a Vacation." Erin wishes to thank Lisa for rescuing her from a life of volunteer anonymity and risking the success of her maiden linguistic effort to the enthusiastic but untried hands of a novice word sculptor.

You can contact Erin at erin@erinwaughworld.com, or knock on the passenger's side window of her son's beater Lumina, where she is jamming to her iPod in sweet oblivion of the oncoming Mack truck of college funding. Erin is just an old person trapped in a well-thumbed Thesaurus.

Dedication

This book is dedicated to Dominic L. Salvagione. Thank you for leaving me with the innate desire to lay my vision down on the printed page. May this book be a tribute to the journey you began but were never able to finish.

"Come live in my heart and pay no rent."

— Samuel Lover

And to my sweet children, Keaton and McKenna, and children everywhere:

To all those who are young in spirit and search for a purpose with passion: dreams are not to be chased. Rather, they are living things that need to be held, embraced, and fed. Always remember to feed your dreams. If you don't feed them, they will suffer and live no more. Have courage. Be the mystery to those who do not understand.

— Mama J

Four Mysteries:

"Three things amaze me,

No, four things I'll never understand—

How an eagle flies so high in the sky,
How a snake glides over a rock,
How a ship navigates the ocean,
Why adolescents act the way they do."

Proverbs 30:18-19 (The Message)

Acknowledgements

With the deepest appreciation, I would like to thank...

Every person, family or friend, who touched these pages with encouragement, support, editing, and creative ideas - everyone who kept me on the right road. You know who you are. I couldn't have done this without you. It ALL mattered.

My editor and friend Erin for turning "funny on the stage" into "funny on the page." For the countless hours of editing and revising and making this book a reality. For incredible patience understanding my thoughts.

My cover designer, photographer, and friend Christos who so generously used his God-given gifts to bring the vision within reach. For the escapades, heart carving, and many good laughs.

My mom and Ray, who made this all possible.

My supportive husband Owen who granted me the freedom to follow my dream.

My wonderful children, Keaton and McKenna, who not only inspired this book but were willing to put these methods into practice.

God, for clearing my head, my heart, and my schedule to make it possible for me to write these pages for Him. For divinely appointing each individual chosen to be a part of this process. For keeping me always in His grip.

~

2 Corinthians 8:11-12

"Now finish the work, so that your eager willingness to do it may be matched by your completion of it, according to your means. For if the willingness is there, the gift is acceptable according to what one has, not according to what he does not have."

Table of Contents

Introduction

Segment One

CHAPTER 1 WHAT IS DATING ANYWAY? 19

CHAPTER 2 WHEN CAN THEY DATE? 29

CHAPTER 3 LOGGING HOURS 39

CHAPTER 4 THE RESPONSIBLE DATER 53

CHAPTER 5 CHOOSING THE RIGHT INSTRUCTOR 69

CHAPTER 6 QUALIFYING FOR DATER'S ED 83

CHAPTER 7 THE PERFECT ONE 97

CHAPTER 8 SALESMEN OR PIT CREW? 113

Segment Two

CHAPTER 9 START YOUR ENGINES! 129

CHAPTER 10 SIGN, SIGN, EVERYWHERE A SIGN 149

CHAPTER 11 BOUNDARY LINES 165

CHAPTER 12 PULL OVER! I'M DRIVING! 185

CHAPTER 13 DATING UNDER THE INFLUENCE 201

CHAPTER 14 EMERGENCIES AND HAZARDS 217

CHAPTER 15 NIGHT VISION AND VISIBILITY 231

Testing and Licensing

CHAPTER 16 PASSING THE TEST 249

CHAPTER 17 HANDING OVER THE KEYS 263

Introduction
Welcome to Dater's Ed!

"Geez, Mom, I'm old enough to drive. Why can't I date?"

I was sitting at the kitchen table contemplating that question as I signed the Driver's Ed log for my son. I was about to promise the world with my signature that my son had in fact driven these required hours with me in the car. Yes, I had spent a good number of those hours gripping the passenger door handle and biting my tongue. Occasionally I had blurted out some vital warning to save us from a fender-bender, like *"Dude! Truck!"*

He had been driving with a permit for just over a year and was actually doing quite well now. His torqued response to my less-than-subtle correction was always the same: "Mom, I know what I'm doing!" Really? Then why is my tongue bleeding?

Eventually I agreed. He *did* know how to drive. I had been sitting right there in the passenger's seat, watching, praying, and teaching him. At this very moment, if he had to drive me to the store, I could calmly ride along and look at the scenery. But dating? You want me to hand over the keys to dating? That's another story. How on earth do I sign off on that lack of education?

Will I ever be able to relax when he's out there holding hands at the mall or stealing glances at his girlfriend over a plate of spaghetti? "This spaghetti reminds me of your curls, Mary Jane."

How do I know when he's ready? How will HE know when he's ready?! As I flipped through page after page of "Supervised Hours Driven" in the driving log book, the answer began to form itself. I had been present for every mile, every brake squeal, and every bumper-threatening ride through our quiet little town as he learned to handle a two-ton vehicle. The State of Michigan *said* I had to be there — to supervise, to correct, to teach. In dating… there is no state mandated instruction, no license, no test, not even a manual to tell a kid how to safely navigate through the dating maze. Was this going to be up to me?

> ➤ **The average teenager still has all the faults his parents outgrew.**

What if he takes corners too sharply or doesn't see the person in his blind spot while he's dating? Why do kids have to log hours with their parents before they can *drive* unaccompanied, but at some magic age we give them the thumbs up to date with no experience whatsoever? I don't get to ride along as he's hugging turns and I'm left standing, coughing, and worrying in the dust. Where does this little sparkplug think he will get *his* dating practice anyway? Is my student even entitled to a "dating permit"? Wait a minute… Maybe the state *has* given me a way to "license" my kid. *I could use the Driver's Ed system to teach my kid how to keep from hitting the concrete wall of a dating disaster.*

Is there a chance that your child will go through life without ever driving or dating? "No thank you, I don't care for fast cars or hot babes." Sure, there's a chance. And I might win the Daytona 500 next year in my beige minivan. What formal training program do you have planned to hone each of these skills that are so important to your kid's future? I mean, dating and driving — these are two very dangerous, fast-paced activities that require more instruction than a "Read Me" can provide. Unless you grab the wheel, your student will end up dating full throttle oblivious to any performance expectations.

Here's the good news. The Driver's Ed manual provides a perfect instructional parallel that every parent can use. We can slowly let out the clutch and teach our kids how to date just like we teach them to drive. They can earn their "Graduated Dater's License" when they have demonstrated that they can date with all four tires on the ground. We can show them how to determine clunkers from show-room prizes, separate Gremlins from Ferraris. We understand that our own little darlings are being tuned-up, painted, and assembled into their own dating "vehicle." They will become either fully loaded smart machines that handle well and avoid accidents or beater cars that need repair for the rest of their lives. Our student's "safety package" could well depend on how we, as parents, mold them and teach them *before* they venture out on their own. We are "instructors" and "mechanics." We can use common road signs and simple driver's education tools to keep our babies safe and focused on the path ahead of them. Do you want to see your daughter crash headlong into an oncoming street thug or parallel park with the Student Council president? How would you feel if you stood by, silent, while your son accelerated inappropriately into a wreck of a girl, when you had the means to keep him "inside the cones"?

First, let's look at the "why" before we put this vehicle in drive. You might be asking "Do I really want to promote the natural instinct my student has to go looking for "love"? Isn't there some kind of cooling system that can quench this burning force to prevent their spontaneous combustion?" Well, the short and very loud answer is "NO!" Sure, you can examine all the intricate sociological motivations for why your child wants to date — Are they filling a need? Are they not getting attention at home? — but that would require another book and a Ph.D. I don't have.

And yes, we should actively try to discourage premature or *uneducated* dating at all cost. HOWEVER, what is more natural and organic than the desire to be with a member of the opposite sex? It's not even about anything as well-developed as the word "romance." In 3rd grade, when Joey pulls Jennifer's pigtails, he doesn't even know why. He's not planning their prom date — he just wants to touch her hair. As parents, knowing that, acknowledging that kids will form attractions for one another, we accept that *it is going to happen*. What we do then is agree to be the director, the guide, the primary observer so that their inevitable magnetism attracts them to each other gently and wisely, instead of like two buses colliding in an uneducated disaster.

Kids will develop many healthy "non-dating" relationships along the way that a parent can encourage: team sports, supportive friends, church groups, and even with counselors. These too are vital to your child's well-being and self-esteem, but these aren't the relationships we fear. These aren't the ones that kids fret over and lose sleep as they anguish in the night about whether Jordan noticed the bracelet they were wearing that dangled the new "Forever" charm, saved for with hard-earned lawn-mowing money.

As parents, you can ignore the signs or try to dampen the longing by locking your child in the garage, but it won't stall the power train of internal desire. "Watch the way Mimi struts her way past the wrestling team." Teens are going to *want*. They can't help it. However, as a pro-active parent you can do what's in your power to build up character in your children beforehand so that when they *do* begin to pick up speed down the Dating Highway, they will be responsible and educated, firing on all cylinders, not off-roading on two wheels. In order to promote safe, healthy relationships your child must pass Respect 101, attend Understanding U., and graduate from the School of Trust.

➤ Buckle up... It's the Law of Attraction!

When your child was in a portable car seat, you might have driven with two fists clutching the wheel. As your child reached middle school, you loosened your grip, let the wheel glide through your fingers, but you were still in control. You'd been doing this awhile. Could your child learn how to drive by watching you from the back seat? "Bumpkins, I know you just turned 25, but Mommy wants to make sure we get there safe and sound so she's driving." Would any state in this nation issue someone a Graduated Driver's License because they watched their parent drive?

The "driver's seat" is how many adults view their role as parents. Period. "My child needs a parent not a friend." Correct. But one of your biggest jobs as a parent is to teach them to stand up on their own four wheels. You held their hand when they toddled around your first apartment. You clung to the back of their tricycle as they motored up and down the driveway until they pouted, "I do it." You clutched the seat of their Raleigh Flyer until they could ride upright but wobbly down to the corner playground and back. And now, in the natural evolution of "gotta get from here to there," you're teaching them how to drive. Not like a friend (riding shotgun, jamming to your iPod™ with your head out the window shouting "Faster, dude. I gotta dry my hair,") but like a parent. Firmly in the passenger's seat, radio off, windows up, antenna tuned to every object within a quarter mile radius. ("Zach, honey, do you see the Good Humor man pulling out of that driveway? Hitting him would not be funny.")

Are you a better driver than your student? Could you safely and intelligently drive the whole team to the away soccer game in Calgary? Of course. Why? Because someone taught you how to drive. Someone slid over on the huge bench seat of your own teenage training-Buick and said, "Here honey, you try." And now it's your turn. Are you losing control? Yup. That's parenthood. Hang on and buckle up — that's how you're going to teach your child how to date. You're going to uncurl your fingers, slide over and say, "Here's the (gulp) key. Try not to hit a tree. I'll be right here in the passenger's seat, buckled in behind an airbag and a prayer."

Nearly all American parents know the rules of the road. Road commissions in every state have generously planted warning and instructional signs all over streets and highways to help us safely guide our vehicles. Why not use these obvious and colorful tools to help our precious, and still single, teens and pre-teens date defensively? In both dating and driving you want the same things for your child: no speeding, no accidents, no bad influences or distractions, and please don't raise my insurance rates. You thought unsafe driving was expensive? The cost for unsafe dating is enormous.

Here is your roadmap.

The book is laid out in two sections. Segment One (chapters 1-8) defines who's who: the driver, the instructor, the salesman, etc. You will discover what a date really is. *When* a date really is. This segment is equivalent to the initial classroom hours of Driver's Ed. It will explore what teens and pre-teens will face on the Dating Highway before they ever leave their seats.

Segment Two (chapters 9-17) puts your student actually behind the wheel of a relationship. At some point they have to drive, at some point they have to date. Through merit and compliance, they will earn a "dating permit." "Okay, honey, you're in the driver's seat. Can you really merge at that speed?" This section follows the test guidelines straight out of the *Michigan Driver's Ed Manual*. It is designed to cover the varied scenarios, road conditions, and hazards that confront every driver (dater) as they begin their relationship journeys. It will provide practical examples for you and your child to explore together. What do those signs indicate? Why is that boundary line there? What do you mean "my vision is impaired by the oncoming gleam of his smile"?

Model It...

When you see the "Model It..." symbol in the middle of a chapter, it will suggest a visual example that you can use to demonstrate to your teen a real-life example of a driving/dating analogy. Like if you wanted to (HONK!) show them (HONK!) how annoying it can be (HONK!) to sit in rush hour traffic (BEEP! BEEP!) or a lunch room (HEY! HONK!) while someone is constantly (HEY!

LOOK! AT! ME!) interrupting. Practical examples. You are encouraged to create your own demonstrations tailored to fit life in your neighborhood.

🏠 Drive It Home...

To summarize each chapter, there will be a section called "Drive It Home..." where you will apply the principles and concepts presented in that chapter to a real-life example. "Okay, sweetie. You have ten dollars to spend at the County Fair with Jennifer. Do you buy popcorn or two chances to guess her weight?" Again, develop your own examples to fit your own values and personalities, but don't skip this step. This is where you will see the real benefits of "riding shotgun" as their primary observer.

DIA-LOG with your student by asking these questions...

The "Dia-Log" section is where you can ask and answer questions *with your student*. Sit right down beside them and have a conversation. During this "interactive classroom" you can toss intelligent questions back and forth without actually getting behind the wheel. "Jess, what do you think Calvin is hoping to do after he drops out of school?" One of the keys to any successful education is to encourage a student to articulate what they have learned — to hear themselves say it out loud. "Budapest is the capital of Hungary. Force equals mass times acceleration. Calvin will "find himself" as he flips burgers."

🚐 Test Drive...

You will find a "Test Drive" section at the end of each of the Segment One chapters 1–8. This will contain activities for students to complete *on their own*. It will offer brain teasers and suggestions for "logging hours." This section encourages students to use that wonderfully analytical teenage brain to think through something non-electronic.

⛺ Road Test...

There is a "Road Test" at the end of each of the Segment Two chapters 9–17. Here students begin to take hold of the steering wheel and maneuver their way through real-life scenarios. This will challenge them to become skilled daters as they accelerate through some of the most difficult dating mazes — left, right, no turn, back up. Dude — truck!

📚 Read Your Manual!

Each chapter concludes with a story, sometimes profound, sometimes outlandish that will amplify the point of the chapter you just read. The tales will lighten up the tone while still having an important impact. It's a place where you can pull into the drive-thru and order a Slice of Humor wrapped around a Nugget of Truth — call it the Lesson Pita. It comes in two flavors — Burst of Sarcasm and Hint of Reality.

> ➜ **I feel like my teen is diagonally parked in a parallel universe.**

You and your student are about to take a family road trip where you will explore the two biggest questions that might just change the way you view dating:

- What is the definition of dating?
- When should my child begin dating?

Okay, three questions:

- What is my job as the passenger and "Primary Observer"?

Kids are in contact with thousands of potential "dates" throughout their school years. Someone has to guide them, steer them, keep them between the lines and off the curbs. This book is designed to give you a framework in which to teach them these important dating principals, based on something you know very well already — driving. You know how to drive and you know how to teach driving. Dater's Ed helps you apply very common Driver's Ed analogies that can be found everywhere. The book will provide you with specific analogies that you can summon instantly for "on-the-spot advice." It will ask hundreds of questions, some left unanswered, to inspire you to create your own points of illustration. Not all kids are created equal. Not all kids are created equal. They don't drive the same and they certainly don't date the same. Every student will pave his own road. Dater's Ed is the instruction manual for your child's dating test track.

∾

"I don't wish to be everything to everyone, but I would like to be something to someone."

—Javan

Welcome to Dater's Ed!

✦

~

"How on earth are you ever going to explain in terms of chemistry and physics so important a biological phenomenon as first love."

~Albert Einstein

1 What is Dating Anyway?

I still remember my son's beaming face. He couldn't have smiled any wider. I bought him a "ride-in-it" electric car from a garage sale, the dream vehicle of every six-year-old. Two children could fit in the front seats, and its purring electric motor might "vroom" down the street at a whopping two miles per hour.

He may have only been six, but he knew what to do with his sweet new ride. He kicked the tires and filled it with pretend gasoline. It all came so naturally. He had read about cars, spent hours zinging his Hot Wheels down the tracks, and ridden in daddy's big truck hundreds of times. He knew what the steering wheel and the gas pedal did. In just minutes he was tooling down the sidewalk with a new found sense of independence. He had crossed the freedom barrier.

Now I ask you this — was he driving? Yes and no. Sure, this was a car but it wasn't a real car. After all it was plastic, and small, and had a motor the size of a Chicken McNugget™. There was no other traffic besides a happy cheering mommy and some neighborhood dogs. There was virtually no danger.

So what qualifies as "real" driving? Look at these examples:

- 15-year-old on a full size John Deere™ Tractor
- 12-year-old at the wheel of a water-ski boat
- 8-year-old in a bumper car

- 13-year-old in a motocross race
- 10-year-old operating a gas powered golf cart

We might debate the qualifiers but my point is this, each of those examples is clearly a form of driving. Dating, on the other hand is a lot more challenging to define because it can be so much more abstract. Think about how you define dating. What is a date? Can you nail it down to a specific activity or is it more intangible and harder to pinpoint?

👪 Model It...

Look through an age appropriate magazine and play "I spy" looking for hidden dating clues in the pictures and the words. For example, you might see two people holding hands on a sunny beach or read the words "for the perfect moment" as the couple gaze lovingly into each other's eyes in front of a blazing fire. Are they dating? Talk with your student about whether or not that would be acceptable at their age.

In the old days, if you wanted to date Harriet's daughter, you first had to have a conversation with Ozzie. Ozzie let you in and told you his darling daughter would be right down after she "freshened up." You shared a polite chuckle at the silly traits of women. Finally the daughter sauntered down the stairs in her mother's borrowed pearls and Ozzie told you to "Have her home by eleven o'clock young man." He shouted to you from the front porch, "Mind your manners!" He gave you a wink as you opened your car door for your girl, and you give him back a "thumbs up."

That's a date, right? Sure, but is that the only kind of date there is? Hang on... that definition is old fashioned, not to mention pretty narrow.

When you are driving a car, whether you just pop behind the wheel for a quick trip to the corner store in your ratty shorts and flip-flops, or you put on your best suit and motor to church, **YOU ARE DRIVING.** The rules of the road do not change from one trip to the next. Whether you are a distracted mother fishing through the junk in your glove box, or someone's professional chauffeur completely focused on the safe transportation of his passenger, you are driving, you are in charge of that vehicle, you are gaining experience. With that as our gauge, what would be the best way to define dating in one sentence and summarize its real meaning?

Dating is when two people, who are romantically attracted to each other, spend time together.

It does not have to be official; it does not have to be witnessed. It does not matter if it is in the middle of a crowded lunchroom, in a hallway at school, or at a football game. Both people are focused on each other. They are practicing dating.

"What? But this shatters all my pre-conceived notions. What about Ozzie and his pre-date interview? I've never met some of the people my child leans against the locker with. How can I control this?" You can't. Did your own mother know all the times you snuck out to the playground with Joey or met Annabelle under the flowering cherry tree? No. But what you CAN do is accept and acknowledge that this is how it starts and guide your young person into smart "dating skills."

Let's look back at those faint stirrings of young love:

Romantic Attraction. Isn't this really what gets the whole ball rolling? If two people are **NOT** attracted to each other, they probably aren't ever going to date. But when Sarah looks at Michael and thinks he's a "hottie," how can you keep them from being drawn to each other? Is it realistic to think that if you forbid dating until they are a certain age, that attraction and desire will automatically be locked up safely in the garage until then? Good luck with that!

Picture in your mind an average 15-year-old who still asks his dad for rides everywhere. What does he want probably more than anything else? To drive. Even if you tell him he can't legally get his license yet, that doesn't stop the desire. The same is true when it comes to dating. These kids have an attraction for and want to "be with" certain other kids, no matter what we tell them. Attraction is built in. Trying to keep someone from having feelings for another person is like nailing Jello to a tree. And so the dating practice begins. Walk through a middle school and see how many kids are holding hands when they think no one is looking. Ride on a school bus and define dating from the back seat. The label of "dating" is misleading. Do you assume that because you said they can't date until they are 16 that they will just ignore that attraction? That they won't pursue a relationship with that adorable girl at the bus stop? Don't count on it.

Flashback: think about what your parents told you about dating. What were the rules and restrictions?

"That boy is not from the right part of town."

"I couldn't date until I was 18 and neither can you."

"Because I said so."

Do the same rules apply to your kids? Did it work for you? Chances are, if you are reading this book, you did not have the influence of cell phones and the Internet on your dating life. Compared to kids these days, we were raised in a bubble, and **STILL** we managed to find a secluded corner under the bleachers if we desired.

"What if I only allow my teen to go on group dates?" Many parents think there is safety in numbers. This is my favorite mistake. I bought into the concept of group dating like millions of other parents until I saw what it really meant. Here is the picture of group dating: a dark theatre full of ten anxious and energetic teens that have convinced their parents that they will behave and chaperone each other. Would you let ten teens without driver's licenses pile into your SUV and take a road trip together? Of course not. What makes us believe that group dating is any safer? Without a whole lot of instruction or maturity, we might as well let them drive blindfolded towing a load of blind passengers.

So where is your student getting their dating education?

Did you realize that your tax dollars support the largest teen dating service in the country?

The reality is that from kindergarten on, our kids already have a free membership in the world's most prolific matchmaking club. It's called "SCHOOL" and they hang out there for ten months a year. There is no pre-screening and it's free, so anyone can join. Kids are in school five days a week, six hours a day where they can check out hundreds of unmarried, available individuals their own age. It's like a parade of potential "hook-ups." Inside the walls of their education system, students get to hang out with the largest number of singles under one roof than at any other time in their lives. It's not the school's fault or responsibility; it's just a fact. There are often more singles to choose from in school than the number of cars at a dealership. Our kids are not only the inventory on the showroom floor; they are also shopping for the best buy on the lot. By middle school, many teens are already dating in high gear.

I began to look more closely at the relationships of my own two kids, at their friends, and at the chaotic and haphazard way I "dated" when I was a teen. Here is the reality: kids get plenty of unguided experience long before they ever get to high school. In fact, they are "logging hours" and practicing how to date well before they get behind the wheel or "go out." Every time two teens lean against a locker together, they are chalking up "getting to know you" hours. At every middle school "Fun Night" your pre-teen is checking out the showroom floor to see who is worth looking at, and who is looking at them. They are dating with or without your permission. They have forged your name on their "learner's permit."

Each day in their school hallways, kids bounce around like bumper cars banging into each other. They are either willing or reluctant participants in the greatest singles club on the planet, and it's even easier to use than eHarmony™.

Kids don't need streets or hallways to eye the merchandise. Just give them a computer at home, in a library, or a media center. Any kid with free time can speed down the information highway to fill in their membership gaps with Instant Messaging™ (IM), MySpace™ and Facebook™ to find even more options online. It's like sending them to a used car lot every day with no expert advice, dozens of models to choose from, and an open credit line. How in the world do they know which ones are a good investment? Unless our students are educated about dating, they might end up with a piece of junk that no one else wants. Or worse, they might feel like the piece of junk that no one else wants.

Some people might argue that if you haven't made your point by the time your child is a teenager, it's too late. Not all kids are wired the same or travel at the same speed, nor do they all have the same kind of relationships with their parents. I know as well as you do that kids do not want their parents' help when it comes to dating, especially as they get older. The thought of you riding along as their back seat dating instructor would make them shudder. However, if you could send them off, wave to them from the driveway knowing that they have gleaned some good dating instruction from a caring parent, you won't have to tailgate, and the ride will be smoother for everyone. Parents, we will have to back off at some point. Before you get your knickers in a twist, hear me out.

When it comes to your student dating, what do you fear the most?

Let's be honest. Some of these fears are painful to consider. Pregnancy? Violence? Then there is the less bleak but just as heartbreaking concern that your baby might fall in love with a complete Edsel. Are you proactive in addressing your fears by educating your student on dating? Do you just forbid them to date until you can't say "no" anymore? What's the proper prayer for preventing a dating fiasco? "Please don't let my baby hit a brick wall. It's her first time out."

➡ **Airbags will only deploy on impact... what about you?**

Instead, take the opportunity to teach your student about dating long before they will actually need the knowledge — a little preventative maintenance, if you will. Using the Dater's Ed manual can give them some badly needed steering guidance before they crash and burn in a dating catastrophe.

Dater's Ed is to dating what Driver's Ed is to driving.

You spend countless hours in the car with your child. There are road signs everywhere. Learn how to communicate with your child about dating by using what Driver's Ed has already taught us. Dater's Ed can turn your car into a virtual chat room using both car and driving analogies to help your student steer towards better choices. The goal is to provide kids with enough practice before they date to make sure they can navigate the endless variety of dating paths they will encounter. Don't let them out the door before their compass is in good working order.

Throughout these pages, with respect to all adults raising children of any age, I will refer to us as "parents," not because that is what we are, but because that is what we *do*. We *parent*.

So, parents, based on what we know now, take a moment to ponder this question: Has your student dated yet?

🏠 Drive It Home...

DIA-LOG with your student by asking these questions...

How do you think dating was different when I was a teen compared with today?

Dating was... _____

Dating is... _____

🚐 Test Drive...

Student:
In one sentence, define dating.

_____

_____

What is the purpose of dating?

_____

_____

Discuss with your parents the differences in culture, options, and technology that kids today face versus when your parents were dating.

You are Sherlock Holmes. Here is a mystery to solve.

Jack & Jill went up the hill to fetch a pail of water... Were they dating?

_____

Why or why not? List all the evidence.

_____

_____

📖 Read Your Manual!

~

"Piglet sidled up to Pooh from behind. 'Pooh!' he whispered. 'Yes Piglet.' 'Nothing,' said Piglet, taking Pooh's paw. 'I just wanted to be sure of you.'"

—A.A. Milne

~

"It takes a minute to have a crush on someone, an hour to like someone, and a day to love someone — but it takes a lifetime to get over someone."

—Author Unknown

"If this is a crush, then I don't know if I can take the real thing if it happens."

—Author Unknown

When Can They Date?

If you have ever attended the International Auto Show in Detroit, Michigan, it is an amazing event. Each year automakers from around the world display their finest prototypes, slick new vehicles into which they've invested enormous amounts of time, money, and research. Thousands of people hover and gasp around perfect, shiny specimens of the most sought-after vehicles in the world. It is the first time these cars have ever been viewed by the eager public.

Imagine taking your 13-year-old son to the show. When you arrive the place is packed, you can barely get in the door as you squeeze up against thousands of impatient visitors. Finally they take your ticket, and you and your son burst into the showroom bombarded by sights, sounds, and smells that overload your senses. You don't know which way to turn.

Each concept car is better than the last. You round the bend and there it is, your son's dream car. His eyes pop out of his head. He barrels his way through the crowd until he is face to face with his heart's desire: a gleaming black Hummer with 760 horses and velvet seats. He wants to get in it and go, go, go… and he can't even drive. You turn to your son and hand him the keys to that brand new vehicle with his fresh drool on the window. You grin, pat him on the shoulder, and say, "It's all yours!" He climbs in, turns the key, hits the accelerator and speeds off out of sight.

Ya think? Of course not! Who would trust an inexperienced 13-year-old boy with something that valuable? He's never even driven before and you'd hand him the keys to a million-dollar prototype? Not on your life! That's my point. So what does it take to qualify your child for their first date?

> ➡ **Your student is part of someone else's learning curve.**

That shiny new Hummer is not worth nearly as much somebody's precious teenager. What parent is going to trust your child with their child, a "possession" that they value far more than their car? At some point, another parent will hand over their sweet offspring to the custody and protection of your baby teen. Do you expect that adult to give their daughter Jennifer a hearty pat on the shoulder and say, "She's all yours, take her for a spin!"? How exactly will your student do on their first lap around the track? What are the rules? And how do you know if he's passed the test?

Here are some questions to ponder that will help you implement this Dater's Ed manual and determine the level of need with a more structured curriculum to get your student on track:

1. What evidence is there of your student wanting to date? (Wearing cologne, spending more time on the phone, grades slipping, etc.)

2. How would you know when your student is romantically attracted to someone?

3. In what ways have you already given your child the permission to date?

4. What might be missing from the conversations you have had about dating so far?

5. What will you say when your student asks, "When can I date?"

Most adults I have interviewed do not have well constructed answers to those questions, especially the last one. The response is often vague or simply avoided. For those that do have an answer, the knee jerk reaction is most commonly "16." Why? Should it be a constitutional right for every child at that age? Are all kids ready to drive at 16? I think there is a better solution, and it is as individual as your child. When will your child be ready? Not until they're ready. Period. With Dater's Ed you will help them discover that time frame together. The real question is, "What are we doing to prepare them now?" How much time have we invested in their dating education? What will their dating graduation party look like?

> **You can date when I say you can date...
> And that's final!!!**

When do we start the long journey of the dating drama with our kids? A ten-year-old is not too young (or too old) to absorb the ideas on these pages. Neither is a 16- or 35-year-old for that matter. This is an ageless analogy that anyone can apply. Whatever the age, I will refer to all individuals investigating the prospect of dating in this book as "students." After all, when you learn to drive you are a Student Driver. This book is intended to be a training manual and to provide our students with a map to keep them on the right road. It is also meant to keep parents from spinning their wheels.

Restricting kids until a certain age is certainly a common solution ("You can't ride in a car with a boy until you're sixteen,") but this does not address the way they feel. ("Ok, mom, I'll just wait till you're not looking.") And if you've ever met a teenager, how they feel is **EVERYTHING**. If the opportunity presents itself to be with someone they like, which it will in school, your kids are logging plenty of hours of unsupervised dating. By the time they graduate from high school, this instruction might be too late to have any lasting impact.

What about spending time together? Can we restrict that as well? Let's not fool ourselves. A lot can happen before the bell rings for class. Kids have plenty of opportunity to hang out with someone they like. Do you really believe that just because you said "no" to dating, that will be the end of it? If the desire is strong enough and the pros ("But I get to see him!") outweigh the cons ("So what if my mom gets mad at me!"), they will find a way... with or without your permission.

Here is the shocker... it is likely that your student has already been engaged in dating practice based on the definition in the last chapter. In fourth grade, I got a kiss from Bruce at recess when I gave him a creepy-people bat that I had made just for him. It was official. We were "going steady." We were spending focused time together. By the time kids finish elementary school, they have been exposed to the primary basis of dating. It is as simple as flirting on the playground. They are already forming dating habits and ideals with no guidance or instruction. Their dating education is well on its way.

There are plenty of books about dating once your baby is in a serious relationship. I have listed several resources on my website http://www.DatersEd.com. However, dating education should be fun and not consume their world. Taking Driver's Ed doesn't interfere with their schoolwork, and dating shouldn't either. Students park their car in the school lot and go in to class, right? They'd look a little weird taking their car to Language Arts. Students should focus on academics when school is in session. They don't always do that, but they should. They might have to adjust their schedule after school or on the weekends for Driver's Ed, but not by much.

Dating is no different. If they are stressed out with all the time they spend focusing on another person, they may need to slow down. Everything in moderation. The more practice they have in developing healthy relationships before dating, the easier it will be to stay balanced and not obsess. They can begin to realize there is plenty of time. Dating should not be considered a drive-thru to satisfy their hunger pains.

This is where the rubber meets the road. Picking a "date" (as in October 3rd) for your student to have their first "date" (as in Prom—senior year) will be next to impossible. Oh, you as the parent can choose a momentous occasion like this for "my baby's first date," but chances are good that your student is way ahead of you. Like the child driving the mini-electric car, they already have some dating experience. It is the *level* of experience that we want to try to control. Parents, I hate to break this to you but… they are already getting a crash course in relationships. If your child is in school, they are already on the dating bus. Probably right now they have someone on their mind that makes them "twitterpated" or "floats their boat" or "knocks their socks off" or they think is "a hottie." Sure, you might think of it as a crush but what's the difference between a crush and a date? It's getting someone's reciprocated attention.

No matter what you call it, "dating," "courting," or even "going out," when a person has their first date, it is most likely very random and not based at all on their abilities or head smarts. Parents can set age limits ("You can go to a movie with a boy when you're 15-and-a-half") and set boundaries ("You must be home by 11:00") but the bottom line is… if kids really want to bend the rules, they will. You can't watch them 24/7. Besides, is that the full time job you want?

When you are trying to determine when to start their training, here is a critical question: at what age is a student no longer influenced by their parents' suggestions?

• Circle one: 10, 13, 16, 18, 21, 25, 49, 81

Choosing the "when" is not as black and white as driving across state lines. In fact, it's more like trying to pinpoint when they crossed over from an adolescent to a young adult. It's a progression that will cause you to wake up one day and say, "When did that happen? Just yesterday you were riding in a mini-electric car and saying girls have cooties!"

Are you worried about your fifth grader? You might think that worrying about a ten-year-old dating is a bit far fetched, but it is the new reality. Chaperone one elementary school field trip and you will see plenty of evidence of "mutual admiration" between two students. A boy will tap a girl on the shoulder then run back to his buddies and laugh. Then do it again six more times while she squeals and tells her girlfriends what a dweeb he is. That's dating in the making. Oh, they are practicing all right. Somewhere in their minds they have already revved the engines and are cruising towards the real thing. Run fast, oh parents! Jump in beside them and buckle up... you are in for the ride of your life.

🏠 Drive It Home...

DIA-LOG with your student by asking these questions...

What does dating mean to you?

_____

Who can you date? _____

What are the moral, physical, and emotional boundaries?

_____

When can you start dating? _____

Where are you allowed to go? _____

_____

These questions should have solid answers before your student starts actively dating. As you apply the concepts in this book, you will be able to address these questions with confidence.

Test Drive...

Student:

List five examples of why another adult would trust you to date their student?

1. _____

2. _____

3. _____

4. _____

5. _____

Give both a good and a bad example of students you have seen "dating" based on the new definition using only first names or initials.

_____

_____

_____

Approximately how old were the students involved?

_____

In your opinion, was their kind of dating appropriate for you? Explain.

_____

_____

_____

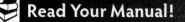 **Read Your Manual!**

Q: How do you decide who to marry?

"You got to find somebody who likes the same stuff. Like, if you like sports, she should like it that you like sports, and she should keep the chips and dip coming."

—Alan, age 10

"No person really decides before they grow up who they're going to marry. God decides it all way before, and you get to find out later who you're stuck with."

—Kirsten, age 10

Q: What is the right age to get married?

"Twenty-three is the best age because you know the person FOREVER by then."

—Camille, age 10

"No age is good to get married at. You got to be a fool to get married."

—Freddie, age 6

Q: How can a stranger tell if two people are married?

"You might have to guess, based on whether they seem to be yelling at the same kids."

—Derrick, age 8

Q: What do you think your mom and dad have in common?

"Both don't want any more kids."

—Lori, age 8

Q: What do most people do on a date?

"Dates are for having fun, and people should use them to get to know each other. Even boys have something to say if you listen long enough."

—Lynnette, age 8

"On the first date, they just tell each other lies, and that usually gets them interested enough to go for a second date."

—Martin, age 10

Q: What would you do on a first date that was turning sour?

"I'd run home and play dead. The next day I would call all the newspapers and make sure they wrote about me in all the dead columns."

—Craig, age 9

Q: When is it okay to kiss someone?

"When they're rich."

—Pam, age 7

"The law says you have to be eighteen, so I wouldn't want to mess with that."

—Curt, age 7

"The rule goes like this: If you kiss someone, then you should marry them and have kids with them. It's the right thing to do."

—Howard, age 8

Q: Is it better to be single or married?

"It's better for girls to be single but not for boys. Boys need someone to clean up after them."

—Anita, age 9

Q: How would you make a marriage work?

"Tell your wife that she looks pretty even if she looks like a truck."

—Ricky, age 10

~

"A boy becomes an adult three years before his parents think he does and about two years after he thinks he does."

—Lewis B. Hershey

"Teenage girls are too caught up in being with a guy who's the best for everyone else and not the best for themselves."

—Author Unknown

3 Logging Hours

One cold winter day, my friend bundled up three of her six kids and packed them into her husband's car to go to church. She was dressed in her Sunday best: skirt, pantyhose, and heels. She got behind the wheel ready to head out, but just before pulling away from the curb, she remembered she had to return a pair of borrowed winter boots to her neighbor. She had laid them in the passenger seat right before she climbed in to the car. She grabbed the pair of boots and jumped out of the car to deliver them. She was walking up the driveway, holding the boots in her hand, when the car began to roll downhill. She sprinted after it in her Sunday heels faster than Ginger Rogers could dance backward, but it was no use. The car rolled down the hill, across the street, through a split rail fence and onto a frozen lake. All the while her kids were screaming inside the car, "We're going!" Yes, she was still holding the boots in her hand.

This story had a happy ending. The frantic mother was able to drive the car and her now safe and calmer children off the lake. They chuckle about it now that they're older and their blood pressure has returned to normal. "Don't let Mama leave here without her boots on" is the running joke now, but this could have been a nightmare. The point is that even experienced drivers can have one inattentive moment that leads to tragedy. They must stay alert at all times. The same is true with daters. Teens can wreck both cars and relationships quicker than you can say, "Hey, is that a *car* on the ice?" Freaky things happen in the blink of an eye that can drastically change a kid's future if he or she is not paying attention.

So what does dating have to do with driving? Actually, the Driver's Ed Manual contains the best advice I've ever read on dating. If you change the word "Driver" to "Dater" in the Driver's Manual, you can apply concept after concept to dating practice:

- There is a right way and a wrong way.
- You have to be safe no matter what.
- There are very specific rules to follow.
- The more you practice, the better you get.

Perhaps the most important and consistent rule that is stressed repeatedly throughout our state's Student Driver's manual is this:

A student driver must log 50 hours of driving time. They **NEED** the practice.

In Michigan, a student must spend dozens of hours behind the wheel of a large automobile with a qualified instructor sitting within arm's reach of the steering wheel. That teacher, let's be honest, actually risks his life to sit in that passenger's seat and bark corrections to this terrified newbie driver. Why? Self-preservation — trying to keep everybody inside the car alive. Not just alive, but undamaged. One car accident can ruin your life.

Let's extend the analogy: If it makes sense to log student-driving hours, does it not make even more sense to log student-dating hours? If maneuvering a huge vehicle on these mean streets takes practice and we want to keep our bodies intact, how important is it to log student-dating hours to keep their hearts in one piece? What could be more fragile than a teenage heart?

"Wait, so what are you saying? **WATCH** my kid date?" Well, yes and no. You could just hand them the keys and say, "See ya at 11:00! Be safe honey!" or you could drop Trish off at Brian's house and let them invent their own definition of "hanging out." Does that sound like good, common sense? Just shove your young folks down the driveway and say, "You figure it out. I know you are a sensible and well-grounded in the ways of the world." Instead, you can create events, things-to-do, real-life occasions that will allow these two young people to get to know one another in a setting other than going to the mall or sitting in front of a DVD.

If you fail to plan... plan to fail.

Can you prevent all broken hearts? Of course not, but why not avoid the most obvious disasters if you can? Why not grab hold of that student driver's steering wheel before his Cadillac hits a parked Pinto?

Let's recognize and accept that that all kids are "Student Daters," yes, even yours. Let's accept, also, that **YOU** are held responsible as their navigating co-pilot and will sit many hours as a passenger while they practice dating.

Perfect. Now all you need to do is attach a bright yellow sign to the top of your kid's head and one on their fender that says *Caution: Student Dater* then everyone will know they are in training. Reality check. There is no way my kid or anyone else's will walk around with that big billboard hanging off his or her bumper. There has to be a better way.

In Michigan, a student driver is required to log 50 hours of driving with a parent, 10 of which must be nighttime hours. Every student is different. Some kids might need *twice* that much, and some difficult skills might need more focused instruction. For example, my daughter was terrified of driving on the highway at night, especially merging into rush hour traffic. (And don't get me started on parallel parking.) We had to spend extra hours honing these skills. The number of hours however, is not as important as the quality of instruction that is taking place. As the designated co-pilot, if I am talking on my cell phone or dialing in Oldies radio while my kid is driving, how much am I teaching her?

In the back of our state-approved Driver's Ed Manual, there is a page called the *"Student Driving Experience Log"* where the teen documents the number of hours driven and whether those are night or day hours. (Each state is different but I will use the Michigan manual as the example throughout the book.)

According to our state manual, teens can't get their license until they meet these minimum requirements:

- *They must drive six hours with a paid, certified instructor.*
- *They must log 50 hours with a parent or guardian before a license is issued.*
- *There must be 10 hours of night driving experience completed.*

How would dating change if kids were required to log a certain number of hours with another student before they could actually "go out?" Few kids jump for joy when they find out that they need that many hours of "observed" driving hours to be any good at it. We know better. We have all been cut off and nearly rammed by a teenage driver who just did not know how fast or how big their vehicle was. Shouldn't dating practice be just as important?

➡ Who pays for bad dating decisions?

Driver's Ed is the government's way of trying to standardize what all drivers should learn so that young drivers do as little damage to themselves or others as possible. The Secretary of State booklet says that the parents or guardians are *"often the best judge of your teen drivers' progress, skill and maturity."* That's the sugar-coating. Below that it says, *"They* (meaning the State of Michigan) WILL *"notify you by letter if your teen driver is convicted of violating the terms of his or her Graduated Driver License."* Guess what else? The state also gives *parents* permission and authority to hold back or suspend their teen's license if they are *"not ready to handle certain driving privileges."* Bottom line… the parents are ultimately responsible and they will suffer the consequences of their teen's bad driving choices or lack of experience, and the state wants every parent to know that. Is that not also true of bad dating choices? Who is in charge of their competence?

> ➡ **Very few kids fail Driver's Ed — millions fail at dating.**

The pre-requisite for signing the Driver's Ed Log is simply that you are the legal guardian who will take responsibility for guiding and enforcing what they learned in class and on the road. Now apply this to dating and here is what your role looks like in their dater's education:

- *Must be legal guardian — not a disinterested party*
- *Ultimately responsible for student's actions*
- *Supervise the majority of hours logged*
- *Monitor progress and skill level*
- *Signature required for official approval*

This might sound like more than you signed up for but should your student "date," "go out," or be alone with someone they barely know? Are you comfortable with the amount of "safe" time they have experienced? We all know that rushing in to a high-level commitment can be a costly mistake. Remember, these are young people. They have not done this before. They have no idea what this person they are attracted to is really like. If sweet-faced Janelle stole her last boyfriend's class ring, you might not want to give her your grandma's pearls to wear to Homecoming. It's important for your student to find out about a "potential date" by logging hours before Ozzie sends them off to the Sock Hop.

So where do parents come in? The idea is to expose your student to as many "real life" scenarios as possible in a safe and controlled environment. Do you practice parallel parking between two Mercedes or two garbage cans? Students should spend time with each other *before* they get seriously involved. In other words, Ali must log some hours with John somewhere where they are visible and able to be rescued by the people who will eventually "sign off" on their dating license. That's you, the parents.

Model It...

Take a look around your house and determine with your student which rooms could be designated for logging safe dating hours. Here's how to apply it: rate each room of your house according to "risk factor." On a scale from one to ten, determine what kind of quality time two students could enjoy without inviting trouble. Help them imagine a couple they know from school in each room and whether or not that space would be appropriate. For instance, stand at the door of the bathroom and discuss why this would not be a good place to log hours. "Would it be awkward for you if Janet and Fred spent the evening together in your bathroom with the door closed?" Likewise, have a conversation about the dining room, bedroom, or basement. The key is to help your teen visualize the potential pros and cons in each room. You may even want to consider rearranging the furniture to improve the chances of healthy dating. If you put your family computer in a public space for easy viewing, does it make sense to do the same with a new "couple"?

In the same way that each student has a different driving learning curve, each student will date differently and acquire skills at a different pace. Some "potential daters" will need to log 50 hours, others might need to log 50 days. That will be up to you. Again, the number of hours is not as important as the quality of the time they spend together. In Driver's Ed, the state actually expects them to keep track of their hours. The same can and should be true for Student Daters. Encourage your student to document dating practice hours in a journal. A journal of hours logged can provide some very interesting insights to your student's progress. Logging hours of meaningful interaction with another student can simply be called the "Dating-Log". Here are two possibilities for keeping track of hours and their relative "enjoyment level."

Spreadsheet:
Your child can use their computer skills by keeping track of dating hours logged on an Excel spreadsheet. They can log the actual number of hours themselves and make notes about their time spent. Yes, your student may balk at this quirky suggestion, but you can make it fun. Label each column as an "Event" (like rollerblading). List number of hours spent together for that event in the first row. Then your student would label the rows with traits that are important to them: Fun Rating, Kindness Rating, Talent Rating, Respectfulness Rating, etc., alternating each row with a place for comments. After your teen has attended an "event" with their date, have them jot down some notes about his or her experience. Rate the date (on a scale from 0–5) for each category that was important to your student. Make concrete comments about how it felt. (You can't know where you're going until you know where you've been. It's great to look back at these in the future.)

A sample spreadsheet might look like this (the title/header of the Excel "book" is "Chris"):

Event:	Rollerblading	Picnic
Hours:	2.5	1.5
Fun Rating:	2	4
Comments:	bored after 1 hour	best part-Frisbee
Talent Rating:	4	1
Comments:	Can solve Rubik's in 1 min.	potato salad gross

Your student can even use the "sum" and "average" functions for each row to see the bigger picture. (They know how to do this in Excel. They just won't tell you because then you'd want them to do your taxes.)

Journal:
For more privacy or a non-technical method, your teen may want to use a diary or a spiral notebook. They idea is for your child to be able to look back at their own written word as a reference and learn about this person they like and their relational experience.

Here's an example of a journal log. Carli might write: *Tuesday, Michael and I made cookies from scratch. He's so dreamy! We went online and downloaded a recipe for oatmeal cookies together. It was so awesome! He ate most of the cookie dough, but when they were all done, he took a plate of warm cookies to my mom. He said my eyes are like cinnamon. He's so funny! (Three hours together).*

There are many creative ways to log hours with a "potential date" and to learn a few lessons along the way. Remind your teen that this is very subjective. Funny to one person is not so funny to the next. It is not about passing judgment but evaluating compatibility. You do the same thing when you shop for a car. You buy what best fits your style, personality, and needs.

Model It...

There are hundreds of personality profiles and "get to know you" quizzes on the Internet that can add deeper insight into your potential date. If you Google "personality profile" it will bring up literally thousands of "tests" that you can share with your friends and family. MySpace™ in particular has quizzes and polls that my daughter and her friends send to each other all the time. (What Color is Your Soul? Are we true friends?) Print off several of these for your student to complete and an extra copy for them to give to their potential date. This is a great ice-breaker exercise for the two students and will count towards hours logged. Oh, what they will learn.

Fill in the profiles yourself or as a family and discuss them with your student. Get a sense of how they feel about the accuracy of the results.

✦ Be sure to read the quizzes and profiles thoroughly ahead of time to avoid advocating inappropriate material.

Let's say your son Adam invites Jessica over to help clean out the garage on a sunny summer afternoon. This is their fourth time getting together. His journal entry might read as follows:

Describe the dating conditions: *Spent four hours with Jess cleaning the garage. Or should I say "I" cleaned the garage while Jess whined and complained that the dust hurt her eyes, and she was thirsty, and "come ON, Adam, I'm bored." Finally, she took a broom in her manicured hand and the next thing I know she's sitting on her rear-end petting the dog.*

How did that make me feel: *That was four hours spent with Jessica I will never get back. I think she was really expecting me to do it all for her. I guess we just don't have that much in common.*

Aren't you glad that Adam discovered these wonderful qualities about little Jessie early in their dating game? Now they can just focus on a friendship instead. As students log hours in a safe environment, they learn early on whether a person is "dating material" or should just remain a friend. Your student can choose any of these methods of logging hours or design their own.

Model It...

Why not invite the other student over to play board games with your family? Not only could this be fun, but your student might also discover whether the date is a good sport, whether he's a leader or a get-along-go-along type, whether he's verbal or physical, or even what makes him laugh. Use this as a talking point on how to log these hours by whatever method they choose. Guide

them through the first few documentations (logs) until they don't need (or want) your help with it.

As kids demonstrate good dating habits, parents and guardians will be able to put more trust in them. You can't watch them forever. You may want to, but you have to let them out of your sight at some point. Wouldn't it be better if you could trust them to navigate safely through the dating minefield because they proved themselves in training under "friendly" conditions? The key is intentional, structured time together, not just "hanging out."

> ⟳ **Remember, "Hanging out" = "Parking"**

This manual contains carloads of things to do for "potential daters." There will be activities and suggested "conversation starters" in later chapters. Most ideas can be modified for age-appropriateness and can be used as simply a starting point — they can expand any idea to fit their lifestyle. Encourage your student to come up with his or her own ideas that are tailored to their own interests. They are more likely to take ownership of the process and actually put thought into spending structured time with someone when they design their own events.

Learning how to date is a skill just like driving. It requires education followed by plenty of practice.

🏠 Drive It Home...

DIA-LOG with your student by asking these questions...

What do you look for in your home that will provide a good space for getting to know each other?

Rooms with the door open or closed? _____

Is the room in the busy path of traffic or not? _____

What is the level of privacy? _____

Describe the seating and the comfort level. _____

_____

Name five things you might want to do on a date?

1. _____

2. _____

3. _____

4. _____

5. _____

How many hours do you think you would need to spend with someone before you felt you really knew them?

_____

What can you learn about someone by watching a movie together? _____

_____

_____

Get your egg timer out for this one! (A second hand will do.) On index cards or scrap pieces of paper, write down fun things two people might do on a date. Throw in plenty of crazy ideas, for example:

- Paint the Empire State Building
- Play hide and seek in a Chuck E. Cheese™
- Milk a cow
- Throw snowballs at helicopters

You have two minutes. Go.

Now... Switch papers. Discuss each activity and decide why it would or would not be a good idea. Talk about how they would get there, who would pay, what you would wear, how long they would be gone... The idea is to open up their imaginations to the possibilities that exist and to teach them how to rationally rule out obvious disasters. ("Mom, can I drive 400 miles to Ohio with two other couples on a Tuesday?" "Sweetie, do you know that I would padlock you inside your room before I would say yes?")

Put all the ideas face down on the table and mix them up. Choose two and see if you can come up with a suggestion that combines both:

Example: Throw snowballs at the Empire State Building.

Playing mix-and-match teaches students how to brainstorm and compromise. Discuss the pros and cons to each combination. "How dangerous would it be to throw snowballs at the Empire State Building?"

Talk about active dates versus passive dates.

- Watching football on TV vs. playing tennis
- Going to a movies vs. going to a community fair
- Buying cookies vs. making cookies

Remind them that no matter how "dreamy" their date is, they might still get bored. And then what?

 **Test Drive...**

Student:
Use pennies to represent ½ hour. Put 100 pennies on the table with a calendar by month. Have your student put

1 penny on each day, week or month to get 100 pennies spent or 50 hours logged. School hours do not count!

If Matt met Heather on January 1st and logged 5 hours each week, in what month would they have 50 hours logged? _____

If each activity was 2½ hours, how many times did they get together? _____

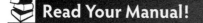

How well would they know each other by then?

_____

How long did it take you to get to know your closest friend?

_____

Read Your Manual!

∾

"A good plan is like a road map: it shows the final destination and usually the best way to get there."

—H. Stanley Judd

"The invention of a teenager was a mistake. Once you identify a period of life in which people get to stay out late but don't have to pay taxes — naturally, no one wants to live any other way."

—Judith Martin

~

"You can tell a child is growing up when he stops asking where he came from and starts refusing to tell you where he is going."

—**Author Unknown**

4 The Responsible Dater

Marge! Look out! I bolted
straight up from a sound sleep in the station wagon as my father
shouted — just in time to see a poodle flying through the air.
In that split second my eyes registered that its pink, diamond
studded collar was attached to a leash. We were traveling
northbound on 127 at the speed of light... through a rest area.
The lady on the other end of the leash had yanked her beloved
Fuzzy Puddles out of the way of our car just in time.

Mom was driving. Dad had probably been reading while all the
kids were sleeping snuggly in the back of the station wagon.
Who in their right mind would design the off ramp of the John
C. Mackie Rest Area *on the left side* of the highway? With a
straight ahead ramp on your *left* to get off? The normal drivers,
those who wished to remain on the "Happy Highway" made a
sweeping curve around the rest area to the right. It probably
made sense to some civil engineer (*somebody* has to graduate at
the bottom of their class). But even as odd as this design was, it
wasn't like my mother had never driven this particular piece of
"Frenetic Freeway" before. We had traveled this same highway
every weekend for years. I can only imagine the looks on the
faces of the weary travelers getting out of their cars to stretch
their legs as we barreled on through. I *have to* imagine it because
at that speed, their faces were only a blur. How could my mom
have missed that?

Some people out there in the dating world are just like that. They are accelerating at warp speeds and cannot see the harm they are about to inflict. They may be taking people out left and right since they cannot see past their own agenda and are heading straight for a brick wall. (Or a flying poodle). Clearly, they have no map, no instructions and no experience to navigate the social landscape. All you can do is steer clear of these "accidents in training" so you don't get hurt.

One of the biggest mistakes made by singles who join dating services is to ignore the basic dating requirements. They jump in, put it in drive, and hope for the best. They basically skipped Dating 101. They believe they are ready for a date when they are barely ready for a Coney and a root beer. They fail over and over again but they always think it is the other person's fault.

➡ **If you got three speeding tickets, would you blame the car?**

In this age of turbo technology, our kids have fast and furious options, including abbreviated relationships. Everything for them seems to come faster and at an earlier age. It's a drive-thru mentality where even social interactions are accelerated. The extent of a relationship might be based entirely on text messages and IM's. Thousands of underage couples have never spent time together except through a computer. Adults date online because it's fast and easy. All ages seem to be missing the foundation for long-term friendships. They don't even take the time to get to know another person fully before they discard them as "not an option." So how do we slow our students down long enough to make an honest assessment of the people in their lives without judging or assuming?

Remember back when you took Driver's Ed? You were probably anxious at first. You became a more responsible driver by taking the classes, learning the rules of the road in a classroom, and by spending many, many nervous hours behind the wheel with a supervisor in the passenger seat, who was even more nervous. As a Student Driver, you actively participated in your own education until you were able to pass the test and get your license. This manual provides the equivalent program for Student Daters.

Driver's Ed has already shown us how to turn an inexperienced "newbie" into an actual automobile driver. The State cannot afford to send uneducated young teens out on the road to put themselves and others at risk. Before anyone operates a moving vehicle, he is required to know what makes it work. "What happens when I push this button? What does this dial mean? Where do I put gas in the car?" After years of practice, adults do this automatically.

Model It...

Most experienced drivers know their cars inside and out. Before we get into them, we have a routine, a subconscious safety checklist we run through before we even turn the key. We keep track of things like when the oil needs to be changed and whether or not the tires are bald. We know if someone put a scratch in the door and look in the back seat to see if our groceries and briefcase are still there. We can tell from the wobbling steering wheel when the wheels are out of alignment, and we cringe at that ear-piercing screech when the brake pads are worn. The next time your student gets into the car with you, ask them to perform a safety check with you and discuss what they felt was important to look for. Did they actually get out of the car? Did they rush and miss critical check points? Talk about what a dating safety check might look like and how often it needs to occur.

Friends, family, and even strangers play a huge role in both a student's driving and dating success. We rely on observations and even advice from others to keep our kids safe and responsible because most kids have a skewed perception of their ability to handle certain privileges. They borrow lines from TV shows and from kids at school. They are convinced they have it all figured out. Do they? What kind of training, influence, and exposure have they had? What situations have they navigated successfully that gives you confidence in their judgment? Are they putting the cart before the horsepower?

> ➡ **It's tough to see when your own brake lights are out.**

Without explanation and guidance, students cannot be responsible for knowing everything that could possibly go wrong as a driver. It is reasonable to assume that dating is even more complex and unpredictable. Do we expect them to be able to change a flat tire for the first time without some help? Do they possess the right tools and skills to know when to leave a party if it becomes unhealthy to stay? It is our responsibility to cover all the basics before we let them shift into gear.

Adults have a level of awareness that is far greater than that of a child. That is precisely why parents are in charge! Has your student mapped out the kind of person they want to date? Probably not. They just live by the feelings of the moment ("Omg! He just looked at me and smiled!") and not necessarily the facts (he was holding another girl's hand when he did that!). The friends they choose and the friends that choose them might be one good gauge of the kind of people your student is drawn to, but it might miss by a mile the kind of person they will have a crush on. The signals your student gives by the way they look, dress, and act can point to others they might attract.

The problem is that most students are not fully aware of the hazards of ignorance or innocence. The lack of awareness of their own signs and signals can lead to disastrous results. Forgetting to use your left turn signal could cause an extreme reaction by another driver whether you were aware of it or not. Does your student even know where his or her turn signal is located? What about other, more personal, signals? If your daughter shows too much cleavage, even if she does not realize it, that does not change the "chin on the floor" reaction of someone looking at her. Let's help them get to know themselves and their potential dates better before we send them off to the races.

> ➡ **Their driving record stays with them a long time. Their dating record stays even longer.**

Speaking of races, it is a fact that Indy 500 drivers are probably the safest drivers in the world in spite of the speeds at which they travel. They always know the condition of their cars before they drive. They take meticulous precautions and spend years practicing at speeds over 200 mph. They worked their way up to this. Even Dale Earnhardt, Jr., didn't drive his first Chevy on the oval track at 100 mph. Smart student drivers don't drive fast the first time out; they take it slowly because they are petrified they will crash this huge vehicle. They should not even think about getting into a car until they can handle the demands of the road and can safely operate a two-ton box of moving metal. The same is true for a relationship. If you can't steer, don't drive.

Model It...

Pick two familiar locations near your home that you drive to frequently (school, grocery store, mall, etc.) and ask your student to draw a map to both places that includes the name of each street. Discuss the level of awareness you need to have in driving and dating and what can happen when you aren't paying close attention.

Ask your child to name two things that signify his or her readiness to navigate the dating scene.

1. _____

2. _____

How do you know your car is in good condition to drive? Having a routine checklist is just as important to the safety of a car as the skill of the driver; one without the other is irresponsible. Mario Andretti checked his seat belt and tire pressure before he ever started his engine. But even Mario's car never talked to him. Students cannot depend on their cars to communicate problems directly to them. They have to take the time to look themselves. Similarly, they cannot depend on their date to identify every problem in their relationship. They often have to figure that out on their own.

Once you have determined the condition of your car and understand how things work, you learn to drive. However, just because a student drives well on ordinary city streets does not mean they know how to handle rush hour traffic. By logging miles in a variety of situations, they will have a much better idea of their own ability to drive and date. Teach your student how to use the gauges they see in a car as a prompt to evaluate where they are headed. It is difficult and illegal to turn the odometer back on your car. It is impossible to undo bad dating mileage.

 Drive It Home...

DIA-LOG with your student by asking these questions...

Our cars have a variety of visual reminders to keep drivers safe and on course. You can use the same gauges to compare the driving world to the dating world. Use these commonplace analogies to initiate a "dating discussion" with your student any time they get in your car with you.

Fuel Gauge:

Talk about a time when you or someone you know ran out of gas. Explain the stress level that it creates. Ask your student what they would do to avoid running out of gas. Compare that to the challenge of staying "sane" on a hectic day. How easy is it to become irritable when you have maxed out your energy?

- Have them play back the events of the day.
- How much time did they spend refueling (sleeping, eating right, exercising) this week?
- Are they running low on energy? Do they have a good read on how many more miles they have to go for the day? For the week?

This is a great time to talk about moderation and the time commitment in a relationship. There may not be enough hours in the day for all they think they can accomplish. Have them set specific limits on the amount of time devoted to potential relationships. Consider a reasonable amount of time to be focused on another student during week days, school nights, weekends etc.

Cell Phone _____ minutes/day

Texting _____ minutes/day

In person _____ minutes/day

IM'ing _____ minutes/day

Other _____ minutes/day

Windshield:

It is critical to have a clear windshield to see where you are going. Have your student tape a magazine picture of someone attractive on the windshield facing the inside of the car. Have them sit in the driver's seat.

1. Ask them if they like the view out the windshield.

2. Ask them to describe the pros and cons of driving with an obstructed view.

Explain that even though that photo is a glossy bit of "nice to look at," it completely blocks the line of sight, and the distraction will inevitably end in disaster. Sometimes a cute crush can have the same effect. Is your student's view obstructed by an attractive picture or can they see the full perspective?

The Horn:
Honk your horn in the school parking lot a few times and watch how that embarrasses your student. Tap the horn inside your garage and see if that is annoying.

Do you know anyone that is as loud or irritating as the horn? _____

Our voices can be like horns. We can certainly use our voices to shout a warning, but drawing attention to ourselves by being loud is not necessarily a good thing. Road rage is scary but usually short-lived. Verbal abuse from a date is never healthy. Describe and discuss verbal abuse ahead of time so your student recognizes it.

Talk about:
- Swearing
- Name calling
- Disrespect
- Humiliation or slander
- Gossip or backstabbing

If your student **DOES** find themselves in a verbal conflict, suggest a good rule of thumb: As the heat of an argument goes up, the lower your voice should go. Then the feet should move twice as fast. Save the "loud" for laughing.

Brakes:

As you drive slowly on a side road, tap the brakes repeatedly and ask your student if that jerking motion is aggravating. Learning to brake gently is a skill. It might be the difference between hitting the mailbox or not. The decision between just slowing down and slamming on the brakes is made in a split second. Knowing WHEN to slam versus tap only comes with practice. What happens if you wait too long before braking? Trouble. There will be bark in your bumper. What if you are riding in a car or cruising in a relationship with someone who is not willing to use the brakes? It might be more than your hood that gets dented.

Discuss the situations that would require braking in dating:

- Your date comes on way too strong
- Her cell phone rings constantly
- Your date wants to see you every minute of the day
- Discuss the difference between slowing down and slamming on the brakes.
- What if you are asked to do something uncomfortable, or illegal, or unwise?

Have your student memorize a line that they can use in any tough spot: "I think I'm going to be sick." "There is something in my eye," or even "I have really bad gas." They can head to the bathroom, lock the door and think about what to do next: make a call, leave, have someone come and get them. If they are not near a bathroom, they need to be. It is always a good, locked place to collect your thoughts. (Or read a magazine.)

Doors:

We take doors for granted. We assume our car doors will let us in and out of our vehicle when we click the remote on our key chains. Your student may not know the frustration of being locked out of his own car or worse yet, locked in. Sometimes after a car accident, there is no exit. It can be more than just frustrating — it might be downright life-threatening to be unable to escape quickly. Being trapped in a place where they do not want to be or forcing their way into a questionable situation can put your child in serious jeopardy.

- What is your exit strategy?
- How do you actually get out of a situation like an unsafe party?
- How do you escape an unhealthy relationship?

Talk about feeling trapped at parties, in relationships, or even less formal circumstances: your student runs into a bad crowd at the mall. Discuss a code that will let you know that they need a quick exit or rescue when they call. For instance, if they call and ask if the family pet is ok, then that is your secret code to drop what you are doing and go get them. Plan ahead. Have a *key phrase* that you share with other family members in case your student calls for help. Remember, they are not always in a circumstance where they can speak freely. "How's Bowser?" might be the difference between safe and unsafe.

What is your family's "Key Phrase": _____

_____

Mirrors:

Have your student sit in the driver's seat while you stand behind the car. Let them tell you when they can see you and when they can't as you move around. Old relationships and unpleasant history can sneak up behind them quickly if they are not paying attention.

- Is there any unfinished business lurking in their rear view mirror?
- Are any old relationships still hanging around?

Have them read the words on the passenger side mirror while you are driving. "Objects are closer than they appear." Sometimes people are closer than they appear. Remind them that not everyone walks away easily from a relationship. Teenagers notoriously hang on to crushes and obsessions, even when the other person is no longer interested.

1. What will you do when the student you broke up with still sits with you at lunch uninvited?

2. What will you do when your "ex" harasses you with text messages?

3. What if your new boyfriend's "ex" pesters him while you are together at McDonalds?

How each person responds is a reflection of their maturity in handling tough situations. Talk about options when they are caught off guard or can't seem to put the past behind them. Your student may be old enough and mature enough to handle the majority of tight spots on their own.

They might try any of these options to deal with the issue:

- Talk privately to the person and express their feelings with a request to be left alone.

- Ask a third party adult to help communicate the situation.
- Write a letter to the person if the situation is hostile and blown out of proportion.
- By phone, be clear about the expectations.

Unfortunately, there always exists the possibility that someone might cross a serious line about which you as a parent would want to be informed. Define those lines with your student:

- Any threat of physical or emotional harm to themselves or another
- Any involvement in criminal or illegal activity
- Bullying or harassment

✦ If they are not apt to come to you, determine in advance a safe adult who will accept that responsibility.

Safety Check:
It is important to perform a mental checklist before your student even turns the key.

Now what???

What will you do when you get to your date's house and their parents aren't home? _____

_____

Describe the options you have if you discover that the group of kids in the car with you has been drinking.

_____

Test Drive...

Student:
Let your student create a list for evaluating whether any particular situation is safe, so that they are more prepared for what might be around the next corner.

Check List Ideas:

Who...
If your child is with a group, get the cell phone numbers of at least two other people who will be with them. If it's just one person, get his cell (or his parents' number) and make them promise that their phones will be on. If there is a party at someone's home, call the other parents to confirm that there really is a party and find out who is invited.

What...
What is the itinerary? Are you going anywhere after the movie? Ask "then what?"
Define the word "NO" and the discuss peer pressure that follows when you do say "no."
✦ Give them permission to blame you if they need an excuse.

When...
Define your student's curfew. What does it really mean? In the door? In the driveway? In bed by 12:00? Whose watch is the definitive one? (Wrist, cell phone, wall clock?)
How often can you go out with a person and how long should a date last?

Where...

> Agree to call home before you change locations —
> "ASK FIRST"
>
> What places are off limits? "Can I hang out with
> Chunk and Fruit Loop at the Tattoo parlor?"

How...

> What is your mode of transportation and
> who is driving?
>
> How are you getting home?

The "who, what, when, where, why?" questions cover
the map in most cases but feel free to add more if the
pieces don't add up.

 Read Your Manual!

Rick and Dianne were madly in love and couldn't wait
to get married. However, there was a slight problem.
Rick didn't own a car and Dianne's car was getting old
with more than 120,000 miles on it. Dianne told Rick
she'd love to marry him, but needed to first sell her car
and buy one with fewer miles on it in anticipation of
starting a family.

So Dianne put her car up for sale, but no one wanted
to buy it. This frustrated Rick because he was anxious
to get married.

Finally, Rick told Dianne that he "knew someone" that
could turn back the odometer of her car so that she
could sell it. Dianne was hesitant, but finally agreed.
A few days later, Dianne called Rick with the exciting
news. "We can get married now!" she proclaimed.

Rick was ecstatic. "You sold the car?!" he asked. "There's no need to," she excitedly responded. "Mine only has 50,000 miles on it now!"

5 Choosing the Right Instructor

I turned sixteen in 1974. My driver's license was going to be my ticket to freedom. The open road, me behind the wheel with my coolest friends, no dorks — freedom, baby! I understand now why my parents waited as long as possible to grant me that privilege.

My birthday is in April so I took Driver's Ed in the winter. This meant that a paid instructor, not my parents, would teach me how to drive in the winter. Brilliant move on my parents' part. Why not let the expert, the paid guy, teach a teenager how to drive in the snow? At least in those Driver's Ed cars, the teacher has a passenger side brake, or "survival pedal."

I have one particularly vivid memory of a snowy, driving lesson. It was a cold January day and the roads were ice-covered, so our training was held in the school parking lot. My somewhat crazy teacher set up an obstacle course in a lot that was empty. He placed orange cones around the icy parking lot and asked us to maneuver between them. On the ice. Without knocking them over. I believe Student Driving Instructors must all possess a special blend of lunacy sprinkled with immortality in their DNA.

There was a driveway about 100 yards long leading down to the back parking lot. He asked us to accelerate like mad down this driveway, and when we hit the open lot, he would slam on his extra set of brakes, and, without warning, send the car into a spin. (Apparently, this could not be covered on a written test.)

Each student driver reacted differently. Some froze, some screamed, some probably wet their pants. Others frantically turned the wheel the same direction the car was spinning making the skid worse. Very few kids got it right and even fewer remained calm. I obliterated every single cone out there, so I'm sure I got the highest score.

As odd as that lesson might seem to the sane, it actually taught me to be a better driver. That instructor taught me to navigate on snow and ice, in city and highway, fast and slow, around old people and toddlers. My job was to pay attention and learn what he was teaching, because he was the designated instructor, and I trusted him.

How is your Student Dater going to respond when she hits a patch of black ice? Who is going to slam on those passenger-side brakes? How do you simulate for them the first break up in a relationship? Have them watch Soap Operas? What teacher is qualified to guide them through the twists and turns of Lovers' Lane? Who will slam on the "survival pedal" when they skid?

 Learning to drive with a certified instructor is not only a good idea... it's the law.

To qualify to teach Driver's Ed in Michigan, an instructor needs to meet certain requirements, thank goodness. Can you imagine if they let just anyone teach? The 9-year-old *Need for Speed* expert? The 24-yr-old machine shop teacher with eight parking tickets? Grandma Lou dragging her mailbox? The state government sanctions qualified supervision for Student Drivers until they can drive by themselves. Your tax dollars are hard at work to keep your kids safe. How much more careful should we be in selecting who teaches our kids about dating?

In the *"Road Skills Test Study Guide"* provided by our state, there is an entire section devoted to the certification and expectations of the Instructors. Not everyone qualifies. It even goes so far as to say: *"The examiner is subject to severe penalties"* if they perform their job negligently. *"Improper, fraudulent or unlawful driver license tests"* are considered *"a felony committed under these laws which shall be punished by imprisonment for not less than one year nor more than five years and fines up to $5,000 for the first offense."* They take this pretty seriously, huh?

> ➡ **What if people who gave bad dating advice could be thrown in jail for breaking dating laws?**

When your teen is ready to drive, hiring a Driver's Ed Instructor is not optional, it is mandatory. There is no way around it. They might roll their eyes at the prospect of someone riding next to them telling them what to do, but the bottom line is that it is not up for discussion if they want a license.

Model It...

Take your student out to the garage and ask them to get into the driver's seat — especially if they don't drive yet. Then tell them they are going to drive you up to the mall and you will supervise. Get into the back seat with a magazine and start reading. (Now, don't *really* let them pull out!) Ask your student to describe what is wrong with this picture. (If they answer, "I don't know," you may have a bigger problem on your hands than just their dating immaturity).

Dating advisors are also not optional. They are everywhere. Your kid will not date alone. He will date with advice blaring at him from all sides: shouts from kids in the lunchroom, pouting and glossy cover girls at checkout counters, even beer commercials on TV try to steer them. Kids will listen to any advice that works to their advantage especially if we do not provide a different perspective. Are you powerful enough to tip the scales in your favor?

Okay, wait a minute — parents don't get to hire a dating instructor for their kids. There is no phone book listing for "Dater's Ed Teachers." Most of the advice your student will receive will not only be free and unsolicited, but notoriously bad: "Ally's best friend Chrissie says that if a guy calls you for a date, you should always turn him down the first time. If he really wants to go out with you, make him ask twice. Chrissie should know. She's been to two proms!" (Chrissie also thoroughly enjoys flirting and has never had a relationship survive more than two football games in a row.)

Students get bombarded with quick dating advice from TV, movies, magazines, and the Internet where everything can be solved in three minutes or less. Are these "advisors" qualified to teach your precious child anything beneficial? Sorry but you've been outnumbered.

Model It...

Invite your student to sit with you on the couch to go through their yearbook and your family photo album. As you turn the pages of the yearbook, have them point out people they know that have been in relationships. Put a sticky note by each one until you have 10 or so. Tell them you have to pay $250.00 to hire a Driver's Ed Instructor so you are willing to pay the same amount for a Dater's Ed Instructor. Hand them a check made out for $250.00 (which you will void later). Now, ask them to choose one person they feel is worth the money and write their name in the blank. Have them explain why they chose that particular person.

The photo album has two good applications:

1. For the kids who do not yet have a yearbook
2. To look through long lasting family, friends, or relatives that will make a better choice than the dropout down the street.

Parents are ultimately responsible for, well, everything their kids do. Wouldn't it be nice to have a second pair of eyes sitting in the passenger seat to warn your kid when he is approaching a dangerous intersection in a relationship? "John, I think you and Crystal are headed for trouble." Who would you trust not only to point out hazards but also to help map out the best routes for their journey? "Jennifer, maybe you should slow down with Josh while he figures out what he wants." Dangerous curve ahead.

As far as I know, there is currently no bill pending to enforce a dating law or mandated dating curriculum of any kind. Where does that leave us? We are still in need of good dating guidance for our students. Here is the list of qualifications required for Driver's Ed instructors. Let's draw the parallel for dating and define what we need to look for:

- *A third party qualified by age and experience*
- *Ability to teach all aspects of safety and rules*
- *Thorough in covering a wide range of related topics*
- *Proven track record*

After you read this list, you might be wondering how you will find someone that fits that description. Furthermore, how will you convince your student that they can get sound advice from sound people?

Here is a combination that I have personally found very helpful. No, vital. With all three elements, I believe you have a far better chance of stacking the odds for success in your student's favor. Even utilizing two of the three will put you ahead of most parents. The winning combination for our family is Faith, Mentors, and Books. Let's look at each individually.

73

Faith. We all have faith in something. Faith that gravity will keep our tires on the road. Faith that the sun will come up tomorrow. Maybe even faith that there is something much greater than imposing technology to protect my baby even though he is six foot three and 240 pounds. For us, faith in God and prayer is the Comfort when we can't be in the car or on the date. We know we can trust in God to *always* be along for the ride. Whatever faith you have, it can mean the difference between an evening of cocktails and Clairol versus prayer and peace.

Read the list of qualifications again. Who better than God is qualified to teach all aspects of safety and rules, is an expert in every single topic, and has a proven track record? Certainly not me. God wins in every category of age, experience, and ability. Whatever faith you have as a family will surely be tested in both teen dating and driving. Even those who do not believe in God have been known to ask for prayer when their children are in danger or heading down the wrong path. For many, it is where the rubber meets the road and the earth meets the sky. Encouraging your student to embrace the wisdom and moral compass of your faith is the best introduction to a dating advisor I know. He's always there even when you can't be. Is there a better chaperone than that?

Mentors. Maybe your student has an older brother they respect or an Aunt they admire. It may be tough for your child to picture this, but Fat Matt, their beloved uncle with the capped teeth and perma-tan, used to be quite a ladies' man. In fact, he has been happily married to Rosemary for two years, and she is his third wife. He has done this dating dance a dozen times; he just might know a step or two. (In reality, he has probably tangoed with a dozen women all named after spices, but keep your discussions age-appropriate. Fat Matt's first two wives, Cinnamon and Ginger are the extent of the detail your kid needs to know.) However, Uncle Matt does understand the rules of the road. He has been around the block a few times. He knows the hazards; he can spot a dangerous curve a mile away.

> ➲ **It's hard for teens to believe that a middle-aged bald guy with a pot belly ever actually broke a girl's heart.**

If you were trying to find a driving instructor for your student, you would hire him based on age, skill and experience. The same is true for a dating instructor. Dexter, that whiz kid in math class, is great if you need to know how to find the area of a cylinder, but asking him whether or not you should buy flowers for your date may not make sense.

Model It...

> In a public place, spend a few minutes people watching with your student and point out kids that you know have no driving experience. To make a point, say "How many years experience behind the wheel does that kid have to qualify to teach Driver's Ed?" (Obvious answer — none). Then ask how many successful years of dating their best friend has that qualifies them to give dating advice. Discuss the value of experience by comparing it to something they are familiar with: gymnastics coach, baseball coach, math tutor...

It may not be Dexter the math whiz or Chrissie the overzealous flirt, but *somebody* is qualified to offer sound dating advice, and this is what you should discuss with your student. I know that kids do not always want to talk to their parents. For one thing, we're old. What could we old folks possibly know about the humiliation of a "bad hair day" or the way Marna's heart pounds against her throat when David walks into art class?

Besides, kids just cannot tell us some of the genuine, embarrassing, or intimate things that they really want to talk about. Kissing is not something my son wants to have a chat about with his mother over pizza. Kids need to have people in their lives with whom they can discuss these all-important subjects. It takes two people to date, so even if your child argues that they are ready and skilled, they might be dating someone who may have had a bad instructor or none at all. To keep your kid from driving into a ravine, put advisors in the seat next to him that you trust. And that he trusts.

The person you have in mind might be an uncle, a coach, a pastor, or a cousin. Maybe a teacher, a neighbor, or a counselor. It might be more than one person. It might take a village. It might be Aunt Joan. You would not know it to look at her (82 years old, tends a garden, collects porcelain cats) but during her wild days, Aunt Joan rolled a convertible. In her sable coat, with a "beau" in pinstripes at her side and a Martini on her breath, Joan lost control of her car and, very nearly, her future. She spent three months in jail for this momentary lapse in judgment. Perhaps she knows a little about how not to date. (Or drive, for that matter.)

The point is there *are* people out there who are "qualified" to teach your student the rules of the road, to teach them how to navigate the perils of dating before they slam into the guardrail and wreck a fresh paint job.

Just as in driving instruction, a "dating advisor" should be someone who has proven that they are like-minded with you, not your teen. After all, you have the final say-so.

Books. Kids are hungry for the right information especially if there is a particular topic with which they struggle (and I don't just mean algebra here.) Good advice may not be available immediately. You can't always phone up your dating coach and say, "Meet me for a Mocha Latte at Starbucks. Caroline is acting crazy again."

Many authors on the other hand have done intensive research about the exact thing you've struggled with, and have great answers to tough questions. Look for an author that has all the right qualifications and shares your values. Find one that speaks your student's language. Required reading is a part of any good education. There are thousands of books tailored to every age and topic that will say what you cannot.

Model It...

Search online, in bookstores, or libraries for books on the subject you know would be helpful for your child. My recommendation would be to read each book yourself first. Discuss the value of "fingertip advice" that a book holds and encourage your student to choose one to begin reading on their own or with you. Then, make it part of the whole "dating curriculum" your student must adhere to. If nothing else, it will buy you some time if your student is not allowed to date until they finish the 219 books you purchased.

Ultimately, we must also remind our kids that they can come to their parents for advice. Whether you have been happily married for 20 years, you are a single parent, or you have been married three times, you know things. Things you might not wish you knew, but with all that mileage under your belt, you are a qualified instructor, and an extremely interested party. If your teen crashes and burns, it is not just a distant, weepy news story — it will wrench your heart out. Putting qualified advisors next to our kids in the co-pilot's seat is a crucial piece of parenting.

The older kids get, the less likely they are to be influenced by authority figures. Teens are notorious for having an "I'll do it my way" attitude. If a student does not take his Driver's Ed lessons seriously, the instructor can easily flunk him. If a girl repeatedly acts like an idiot around boys, her mom might ground her until she is 40. Teens only get their driver's license once they log a minimum number of hours with a qualified instructor, and prove their level of responsibility by continuously staying accident and ticket free. Otherwise, take the bus.

Of course, just because we provide fabulous advisors and instructors for our students, it is ultimately up to each individual to accept and act on that advice. I can shout all afternoon, "Turn the wheel! You're driving through a herd of sheep!" If the student does not listen to my advice, the last sound she might hear is "Baaa... thump." And when they do ignore our prudent advice, we should not feel compelled to hand over the keys and fill up their tank so they can dust another sheep.

🏠 Drive It Home...

DIA-LOG with your student by asking these questions...

Ask your student which three people they would trust for dating advice.

Have them write the names IN PENCIL. You will find that they need to modify this list as time goes on. This list can include parents, friends, people at church, neighbors, teachers...

1. Who? _____ Why? _____
2. Who? _____ Why? _____
3. Who? _____ Why? _____

Now, go back through the list with them and ask these questions:

- Would you trust these people to hold onto your birthday money for five years?
- Would you trust them to drive you to the mall?
- Would you trust them to help you with your math homework?
- Would you trust them to plan your next vacation?

The point here is this: Kids often think their best friend is their best "dating advisor." After all, last week, she was the "be-all-and-end-all" of relationships. "Kristine said she can tell a lot about a guy just by the shoes he wears." "Jake told me that Rachel really likes me because I'm the class clown."

Here are some questions to consider in finding a good Dater's Ed Instructor. Discuss these with your student.

- What is the minimum age required to give advice?
- Do they have a good track record currently in their own relationships?
- Can they look at the situation objectively? Or are they too close to the scene?
- Do they share your values and are clear about your concerns?
- Do they have the ability to be honest and open about what they see?
- Will they agree to hold you accountable to keep you on the right road?

Other tips might include:

- Have your youth pastor or priest over for dinner to help build up the comfort level between them and your student.
- Take your teen out of school for lunch one day a month to talk about their relationships.
- Find scriptures and quotes that they can apply to own lives and tape them to their mirror.
- Watch a classic movie together that models healthy romance and "decent" exposure.
- Consider having your teen meet with a counselor or life coach to keep their future in view.

Although these criteria are a good start, together you can always add and modify this list based on your child's personality and need. By choosing wisely in advance, you will help eliminate the chaos that results from too many people giving advice (both good and bad) simultaneously. As time goes on, they may find that they want to remove someone from the list and add someone new.

Once you agree on the best choices, be sure to have a conversation with each Mentor on the list to let them know what to expect ... and what *you* expect. Be clear with them about your values, concerns, boundaries, and when they need to break a confidence. Teens especially need a safe place and an educated ear with whom to share thoughts, dilemmas, and even the occasional crisis. Finally, be sure to put the chosen few on speed dial in your student's cell phone.

 **Test Drive...**

Student:

Chaos on the dating bus.
Let's say you are 14 years old and your state has a new way to teach Driver's Ed with your classmates as co-advisors. They hand you the keys and put you in the driver's seat of a bus for your first driving experience. The bus is filled with 40 kids from school and includes your three best friends. You look around the bus and see most of your soccer team, the whiz kid from math class, and the school bully. You jump in behind the wheel and start the engine. No big deal. You shift into drive and think, "Sweet. This is easy." You put your foot on the pedal and carefully pull out into the street. You are actually thinking you have this under control, so you pull onto the freeway and pick up speed. There is an

18-wheeler barreling towards you that you do not see, but your 40 trusted friends do. They yell out warnings at the top of their lungs. Chaos breaks loose. You hear someone yell, "Watch out!" Another screams "Get out of the way!" A brave soul in the back shouts, "Did your mother teach you to drive?!" In a matter of seconds, you can't understand anyone because they are all screaming different things at the same time. There may be calm and rational people on your bus, but there is no way you can hear them over the noise. The bus and the semi collide. Your insurance goes up.

Whose advice was the best? _____

Being honest about whose name goes on your "dating advisor" list is crucial. Chances are your friends will not lose sleep when they meddle dangerously in your relationships. If somebody points you down the wrong road (turn left at the big rock), it will not hurt them like it will hurt you when those directions turn out to be detrimental. (Sorry about that herd of sheep. How much did your new windshield cost?) Remember, when you are in the driver's seat, you can choose your own passengers.

Revisit this list on a regular basis. Talking through this ahead of time will help you avoid grabbing the first person you see for advice when you feel unbalanced. Knowing the individuals you can trust to give good advice helps to keep the training wheels on until you are steady on your own.

Read Your Manual!

"It is hard to convince a High School student that he will encounter a lot of problems more difficult than those of algebra and geometry."

—**Edgar W. Howe**

"Chaperones don't enforce morality; they force immorality to be discreet."

—**Judith Martin**

"Basically, the only thing we need is a hand that rests on our own, that wishes it well, that sometimes guides us."

—**Hector Bianciotti**

6 Qualifying for Dater's Ed

We had to get there. What choice did we have? I was standing up in my friend's wedding and I could not let her down. Besides, I had been driving in snow my whole life. Five hours in a northern Michigan blizzard? At night? Piece of cake. Besides, where else was I going to wear this gorgeous satin peach dress?

I picked up my overly dramatic friend Liz who wanted no part of piloting through a winter snow advisory, thank you very much. She did consent to ride shotgun if I drove us in her 1974 Monte Carlo. This thing was a beast. It was like driving a building. The further north we drove, the worse the conditions became, and the more Liz scooted down in her seat.

We were only two miles from our destination. We came up over the hill on a road I had driven a hundred times. I knew there was a stop sign ahead, but the blizzard distorted my depth perception. I hit the brakes, the car hit a patch of ice, Liz's feet hit the dashboard, and the beast took over.

Suddenly the Monte "Carload" was sliding on its side in the ditch like a gutter ball speeding straight for the intersection. When it finally skidded to a stop, Liz and I were piled in a Bridesmaid heap, sitting on the passenger's side door. Read that last line again. Yep, sitting on the door — the door handle was poking into my corset. The great beast lived to drive another day (it was barely damaged), but my pride was wounded. All my driving experience and qualifications flew right out the frozen window with that little episode.

Qualifying for Driver's Education
When you sign up for Driver's Ed, you have to bring three things:

1. Proof of Identification: a Birth Certificate that shows who and how old you are

2. Permission from a parent or guardian to start driving

3. Money to pay for the privilege

ID
No two people are alike. Even identical twins have differences (ask someone who married one). We know children mature at different rates. Some kids are still not ready to drive at age 16, while King Tutankhamen ruled Egypt at age 10. (Although I bet he couldn't drive).

In Michigan, students are qualified to take Driver's Ed if they can prove they are 14 years and 8 months old. The Driver's Ed Manual says *"Teenagers under age 18 are required to meet the requirements of the Graduated Driver's Licensing (GDL) before they can be licensed."* The State had to pick some concrete, measurable age. They could have picked 4 years old, they could have picked 24, but they chose an age when most teens would be ready to begin to learn how to drive. *Most.* Not all. Some kids at age 14 years, 8 months are not mature enough to operate a Barbie-Mobile.

Model It...

> Pull out your driver's license and talk about what you did to earn it as well as keep it. Is your student mature enough to begin Student Dating? How do you measure that? What does your student's "dating ID" say about him or her? Do they have what it takes to view this responsibility seriously enough to earn the privilege? Talk about the reasons it might be revoked.

Let's look at some characteristics that make up your student's Dating ID:

Respectful. Every Monday morning, early, the trash guy comes to take away a week's worth of your family's generated garbage. Every Sunday night it is your teen's job to take the trash to the end of the driveway. He has missed the last two Sundays in a row. Pizza boxes spill over the edges of the bin, the lid does not shut, and greasy plastic bags sag on the floor of the garage, inciting feeding frenzies among local critters. How responsible will your student be when it comes to respecting your curfew if he cannot even remember to take out the trash? Will he trip over it and ignore it like he did the garbage bags and say, "I forgot all about it"? "What, is it midnight already? I wasn't paying attention." What a surprise.

Trustworthy. You tell your teen that he must finish his homework and vacuum the upstairs while you go grocery shopping. He is not to turn on the TV until you get home and unload groceries. Later you hear him on the phone with someone discussing the "plot" of a "Lost" episode that was on while you were gone. Will you be able to trust him to do as you ask? If you tell him that he is forbidden to visit a friend's house while the parents are not home, will he comply?

Responsible. You are away at work, you come home and find shards of a broken pickle jar on the kitchen floor, and sweet vinegar splattered all over the floor. Your daughter is in a crying heap in her room.

"Sweetie, what happened?"

"Well, (*sniffle*) I dropped the jar of pickles, and it broke (*sob, snort*) and it was so awful!"

"Are you hurt?"

"No, I (*sob, snort, wipe*)... I just... I wanted a pickle and... now there's juice and glass...!"

"So why didn't you just clean it up?"

"Well, I, I don't know, it just seemed so yucky and I didn't know what to do! (*Crumble.*)"

How will this young girl react when her date drives her to a party where he is drinking? Is she mature enough to make an appropriate decision and then act on it? Or will she just panic and wait until someone more level headed gets her out of the mess?

Hygiene. Your kid eats a bagel on a Tuesday morning, then walks out the door in his smelly soccer jersey to the school bus with black poppy seeds in his teeth. He wants to go to the movies with Stephanie on Saturday, but he can't be bothered to brush his teeth, even with attractive black pebbles in his grill. How will Milk Duds look in his smile when he laughs at Adam Sandler? Does his deodorant still have the shrink wrap on it from last November?

These little maturity questions begin to define your student's level of accountability. Who are they? What is their dating ID? Can they be trusted? A kid always thinks he is ready, but is he responsible enough to drive off the lot into oncoming traffic? Is his tank full of experience or panic? Is his windshield clean or is it covered with a week's worth of dirt and debris?

What does your student's dating ID say about him or her?

Parental Permission
Yep. It is our state law and it's not optional. Your student can finagle all day long to take Driver's Training without your permission, but the State will not allow it. To apply for a drivers license, our state requires that a *"parent or legal guardian must accompany the teen to sign the application. Signing indicates parental/legal guardian approval for licensing. With a Level One License, the teen driver may only drive while accompanied by a licensed parent or legal guardian or designated adult age 21 or older."* That's just for starters. The State also requires that the student log a mandatory 50 hours of actual driving experience with an adult outside of the instruction time.

Are you letting your kid date without your permission? Would you let them take your car without permission? If I discover that my son has taken my car without my unambiguous verbal consent, well, by golly, I guess I will need to take away his cell phone. So what happens if I come home to find my child "out" with "a friend" without my absolute authorization? Believe me, he will be put on more than just a "techno-fast." I hope he likes rotary dialing.

Model It...

Permission is something most kids can grasp. To prove my point, borrow your student's iPod™ or go on their MySpace™ without their permission and see if you get a reaction. Oh yes! They do understand the concept of taking something that's not theirs. Talk about how all the pieces work together as part of the dating privilege: respectful, trustworthy, responsible kids with good hygiene are the ones that earn the permission to date. Feel free to add to this list.

Even if your kid follows the rules at your house, it does not mean that those same rules will be upheld at her friend's house. Just because you have blocked her MySpace™ account at home doesn't mean that she can't access it at Natalie's house while they are "studying chemistry." Am I suggesting it is possible for your teen to drive with their hands at ten and two while you are in the car but on their own they drive with one finger and use the other nine to text message? You bet I am.

There are levels of permission. Even if your son is allowed to take the car, it does not mean that he can drive anywhere, any way, with anyone. If he comes home from an evening with his buddies, and there are 300 additional miles on the odometer, you probably ought to discuss how Canadian casinos were not on your pre-approved places-to-go list. If your daughter brings the car home and the interior is littered with McDonald's wrappers and Avon samples, you might revisit the whole "makeup party in a car" prohibition. It is not just "can I or can't I" take the car. It is where, how far, with whom, can I eat in it, and can my friends smoke in it. (Not if you ever want to leave your room again.)

A parent needs to be involved in their student's dating. No, you do not hover, you do not spy, but yes, you do watch the odometer, carefully. You check the bumpers for damage and you monitor the condition of the interior. These are fragile, flighty, ditzy teens who are absolutely certain that they can "make it" through that yellow light. Parents should be constantly on the look out for potential damage because kids cannot always see clearly, even if the oncoming disaster is the size of a furniture truck.

Kids think they are immortal. "That truck is not going to hit me. I am faster and smarter than that driver." So of course, that is their belief when it comes to dating. "This girl is not going to hurt me. This guy will not abuse me. I am faster, smarter, and more resilient." Well, parents know better. That delivery truck may very well may hit you. That depressed and abusive boyfriend will ruin your prom and maybe even your life.

If my neighbor calls repeatedly and tells me that my son is driving his van too fast, I need to have a keys-in-hand discussion with him and promise the removal of said car keys. If a neighbor calls and tells me my son's girlfriend was moving awfully fast with a local football hero, I probably need to have another kind of discussion with my son, whose ego is about to be crushed.

It is relatively easy for parents to converse with their teens about driving laws and impart driving wisdom. It is tougher to confront them about dating do's and don'ts, but it is equally as crucial. It might be difficult to monitor, but playing ostrich just gets sand in your eyes. The bad stuff happens whether you see it or not. If that truck is jackknifing toward you, looking away doesn't prevent the accident.

We must also be watchful of the more subtle signs that might indicate trouble. If a student's grades begin to fall right as he starts dating a new girl, perhaps they are spending too much time chatting on the web. If your daughter's boyfriend speaks to his mother with cruelty in his voice, your daughter might need a refresher course on verbal abuse.

Levels of permission come with a level of trust. Eventually your son will prove that he can indeed drive to Wisconsin and bring you back some of that good Wisconsin cheddar you crave on a Ritz. And someday your daughter will successfully go to a marching band party where underage kids are drinking, keep her head when all about her are losing theirs, and in fact become the designated driver. Keep in mind, students must build up their level of responsibility in bits. You don't start out driving in an Indy car. Your first date should not be the prom. A student must earn that level of trust. Slow down there, little missy!

> **The car doesn't get the ticket... the driver does.**

Two words in our home have become the mantra for our adolescents and teens. Eight letters that have saved us many sleepless nights and kept our kids (for the most part) out of trouble: ASK FIRST. Our kids must remember to "ask" not "tell" or "assume." They must make any request *first* and not after the fact. It's so simple it's brilliant. (That one is worth writing on the bathroom mirror.)

Parental permission is a constant conversation. If you lend your car to your teen, you will check it for dings and malfunctions every time you get back in it. Do the same thing with their dating excursions. True, they might still crash a mile down the road, but at least you buckled them in and paid the insurance.

Money
Driving is expensive. It cost $250 to take Driver's Ed. The minute we wrote that check, a standard was set. Our kids assumed that we would pay for their driving experience and by extension, their cars, gas, insurance, repairs... We might indeed buy our kids a car,

and cough up the exorbitant insurance premium, but we draw the line at spinning rims and sub-woofers.

So what about dating? Who should fund all that? Is that why parents have two pockets? One for driving and one for dating expenses? (And just exactly where do I fish out the money for college?) If your student has a car, somebody must pay for day-to-day expenses like fuel, oil changes, wiper fluid. So who pays for day-to-day dating expenses? Relationships can cost a lot of money. Does your student have a job? An income? A trust fund?

👪 Model It...

Whenever you are with your student and you pay for something like a burger at the drive-thru or a tank of gas, put it into dating perspective. Example: "Geez, Brigit, I just spent 60 minutes worth of my hourly wage to buy you a burger you wolfed down in 37 seconds." Question: "Was it worth it?" or "Well Nick, it would take me two hours of babysitting to earn what I just spent on your Valentine's Day present."

Consider for a moment a guy who is 14 and wants to take a girl to the movies. Who should pay? Mom? Dad? What if he is 17 and has a job? What if he is 18 and doesn't have a job? Who pays then? Bank of Dad? Does your student really know how to calculate the cost of a date? Sure the movie may cost under ten bucks, but what about the gas money to get there, an oil change, and a car wash not to mention the fashion "T" and the skinny jeans? Dating is not cheap. Investment-wise, it is similar to renting a car: it is really expensive every month and you have nothing tangible to show for it once it's gone. No rebates, no refunds, no guarantees.

So whose wallet will be drained if your student launches a dating relationship? It is important for your teen to know the monetary commitment before they spend your hard-earned cash. Talking through these scenarios with your student can give them a healthy perspective when their date says, "Show me the money."

A cheap date is not necessarily a cheap date

Whether it is your money or theirs make sure your student knows that they do not have to buy, pay, and spend just because their date wants them to. It is not always worth it. See if this is familiar: Your son takes his girlfriend to the prom even though she has not been civil to him for weeks. After a long night of being ignored in his rented tux, she breaks up with him. How many hours of flipping burgers did that corsage and steak dinner cost him? Your daughter saved close to a hundred dollars babysitting to pay for the cut, highlight and "up-do" for Homecoming only to be escorted by a guy that still had grease in his hair from last Wednesday.

Not every family has a "Father Finance" or "Money Mom." Encourage your child to earn as much of their own spending money as possible — for dates or cars. They will assume much more pride of ownership for things they paid for on their own. If that steak dinner came out of Mommy's pocket, it is not nearly as precious as when every delicious bite was earned at his job baling hay on the horse farm. If things come too easily to kids, they never need to make the tough choices, and they rarely learn a thing about value.

Now you might be asking, "What about girls?" Chivalry still prevails and guys still frequently pay for dates. Even when this is the case, however, a girl will often spend just as much money as the guy, only it's on clothes, makeup, shoes, and hair-essentials. If girls are old enough to demand these "necessities" then perhaps they are old enough to wait tables or bag groceries to afford their demands.

A word of caution: girls (and guys) should never feel any sense of guilt or obligation if their date pays for dinner or tickets to the show. Explain to your daughter or son that they do not "owe" their date anything for a plate of pasta other than a "thank you." Polite gratitude is the only obligation. Dinner and a movie is a gift - it is not a barter. Nothing should be expected in return. In fact, in the early stages of a relationship, both students should pay their own way — no strings attached, no blurry lines of commitment. "This is my movie theatre seat; I bought it with my own money. You keep your arm off it."

> ➡ **Make sure you don't feel like your date should get "more" for their money.**

Even as your student and their date politely bicker over the check — "I'll get this." "Oh no, let me." "Okay, if you say so," they are learning a little about how their potential partner handles money. Do they mooch, borrow, loan out, or give it away? Are they stingy, generous, or do they count every penny?

Not all dates have to cost money, of course. Believe it or not, kids, there are plenty of things to do that are very nearly free (and moral and safe). You can play cards or go ice-skating on a frozen lake. You can go to the park or attend a street fair (just don't buy cotton candy from every corner vendor). Parents, just because your kids do not want to spend money, encourage them to get up and do something other than "hang out." Hanging out is the same as parking. Parking on the couch is just not an acceptable "date."

Let's recap. Qualifying for Driver's Ed requires ID (proof that you are old enough), parental permission (proof that someone is responsible for you), and some cash (proof that you can pay for the privilege to learn.) Dater's Ed requires no less. ID (are you trustworthy?), parental permission (did you ASK FIRST?), and some cash (do you have a job or is Bank of Dad funding this excursion?).

Give students plenty of opportunities to learn the rules of the road safely. If they abuse the privilege, it can always be revoked. Schools are junkyards of broken hearts and shattered dreams. Demolished relationships can alter a kid's life. The State mandates what a kid must do (and have) to qualify for Driver's Ed, and they do not bend the rules. Dating "laws" are much less tangible. Just because she turned 16 yesterday does not guarantee that she can pilot a Pontiac. Nor does it automatically mean she can handle a four-hour prom date complete with corsage and after-party. Both driving and dating can be extremely dangerous. There is a reason Driver's Ed uses orange rubber cones instead of concrete posts.

Drive It Home...

DIA-LOG with your student by asking these questions...

What are the three most important things you need to qualify you for dating?

1. _____

2. _____

3. _____

What is your "dating ID"? (List five strengths that would convince me, your best friend, and the principal of your school that you are ready to handle the responsibility of dating.)

My five strengths:

1. _____

2. _____

3. _____

4. _____

5. _____

Where do you see room for improvement?

My five challenges:

1. _____

2. _____

3. _____

4. _____

5. _____

Have a conversation about the lists they made above. Ask them:

What will be your source of income? How do you plan on paying for the dating privilege?

How do you plan on getting to and from dates?

In your view, is dating a right or a privilege?

If chores, grades, attitude are not where they should be, what should we do about dating?

Test Drive...

Student:
If John decides to take Rachel to the movies on Friday night, how much will it cost?

Go online if you don't already know how much a movie ticket is.

1 movie ticket = $ _____

Tickets for 2 $ _____

Popcorn for 2 $ _____

Pop for 2 $ _____

Candy for 2 $ _____

Total $ _____

Here comes the fun part. Regardless of how you get there, someone has to buy gas.

How much is a gallon of gas? _____

How many miles per gallon does the car get? _____

Do the math: How far can you go on ten dollars?

$10.00 gas divided by $___ per gallon = ___ gallons = ___ how many miles

Now, go online and map out the miles from your house, to the other student's house, to the movie theatre, then double it to include both directions. If your parents must chauffeur, don't forget to add the mileage for the additional round trips to drop you off and pick you up. This exercise can be an eye opener. It really changes the total value of one date. You might want to reconsider that trip to the free art fair.

Now add it all up:

Total miles round trip = _____

Divide this by ____ miles per gallon = ____ total gallons needed.

Multiply this number by the cost of a gallon of gas = $ _____

Add this number to the number above for the theatre charges $___ and you will get the total for the evening.

How much total money will be spent on this date?

$ _____

Is the memory worth it? _____

Revisit this page after you have actually gone on one of these dates.

Describe where the relationship is now. If it is over, in retrospect, was it worth the money spent?

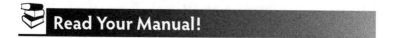

Read Your Manual!

~

"Too many of today's children have straight teeth and crooked morals."

—**Unknown High School Principal**

"The young always have the same problem — how to repel and conform at the same time. They have now solved this by defying their parents and copying one another."

—**Quentin Crisp**

"The will is never free, it is always attached to an object, a purpose. It is simply the engine in the car — it can't steer."

—**Joyce Cary**

"The best way to keep children at home is to make the home atmosphere pleasant, and let the air out of the tires."

—**Dorothy Parker**

7 The Perfect One

My dad proudly pulled into the driveway with a "new" car for my sister and me to "share." It was 1975. I was a senior in high school and my sister was about to leave for college an hour and a half away. We could just take turns, right? Hardly. We battled constantly over whose "needs" were more important. "I have my Sorority Finishing School Graduation this weekend." "But, I'm in the David Bowie look-alike finals on Saturday!"

We were fighting over an ugly 1971 Plymouth Satellite. Not at the top of my wish list. It was Army green and detailed with random rust spots. Where was the red Spider convertible we were hoping for? You couldn't start this homely mutt until you manually released the flap on the carburetor. The charm of opening the hood and poking around with a screwdriver lost its appeal in bad weather. Nobody changed the oil; the gas tank was always empty. We did *not* love this car.

Eventually we sold it, but we both learned a lot about what we wanted in our next ride. (Like, it should start with a key not a screwdriver.) Owning a bad car is rarely life altering. It can be "dumped" with little impact on your emotional well-being. I spent zero lonely nights crying for my lost Satellite. Human relationships are far more weighted, however. People who "fall in love" too fast without doing any research ahead of time can avoid heartbreak with a deeper look under the surface polish of their partners.

Picture in your mind your first car. Chances are, like most of us, your first car was a beater. How much time did you spend trying to make it "sweet"? Do you drive the same car today? Doubtful. In fact, you can look back over the portfolio of your car ownership and compare the cars that you owned in the beginning to the cars that you own now. What have you learned along the way? You probably have a strong opinion about certain brands (GM vs. Toyota) and the options you do or do not like. (I will never be without a sunroof again.) The average American trades in their cars every 2–3 years. What about their love relationships?

➡ **It's not "too good to be true"… it's "too SOON to be true."**

Whether we agree with it or not, we are all judged by our appearances. It is a natural, human thing to do. Someone bumps into you in a mall. You hear him say, "Pardon me." You look up at the guy who just jostled your packages. If he is a dirty homeless beggar, you scowl and back away. If he is a well-dressed man in an Italian suit, you apologize and politely step aside. We have instant reactions to what we see. They are not always correct. That homeless guy might just be an undercover cop. The gentleman in the suit might be a crazy escapee from the local institution. He owns one suit and speaks only in three-syllable phrases. Unfortunately, our judgment is often speedier than our compassion and understanding.

Model It…

Pull out all your old photos of the cars you have owned. If you can't find them, download pictures of the same model from the Internet. Lay them out in chronological order and go through each of the cars with your student. Explain how old you were, how much it cost, the pros and cons of owning each one, and most importantly what you learned from that car and what you would have done differently. Explain how every car is the perfect car only for a limited amount of time… much like most of the dates we've had. Discuss what you learned from the brand and what you look for in specific models. You might want to pull out those photos of former dates too if you have them! (Avoid discussing mileage.)

Students in middle and high school have already begun "branding" themselves by what they wear, how they look, and with whom they hang out. Their names alone have begun to mean something, even if it is a long way from representing the true picture of someone's character. It is the same with car brands: If I tell you I used to own a BMW, you form a picture in your mind of what that car looked like, even if the real one I drove was a battered piece of steel given to me by Uncle One-Lung Charley. The brand itself has a reputation. ("I would do anything to get my hands on a 1964 Red Beemer Convertible.") Your student's name has begun to mean something about them. ("I would do anything to get my hands on…" you get the idea.) What your student drives (a purple metallic SUV) and what they look like (purple metallic hair) reflects something about who they are, even if it is just a superficial quirk (they like purple). Thus, a style is born. The difference between cars and people here is that people have feelings. Kids are routinely judged incorrectly by the way they look and act.

In everything your student does, he creates a brand, a name, for himself. Hollywood has taught us well. In the early 1970's, Michael Jackson was a universal star. Just one look at him and you could see a rare form of talent that fostered idol worship. What do you see when you look at him now? Has the picture changed? Does his face trigger a response that his reputation has altered? Michael Jackson has branded himself by the way he looks and acts and the mention of his name will cause a reaction in people around the world.

How are your students branding themselves? ("Drew is mean. He has a bad attitude and constantly talks trash to the math teacher. At least that's what I heard.") Does your daughter's name have a meaning beyond what you intended? You might have named your little girl "Mary," meaning "star of the sea," but now she's known as "Mary, star of the 'see how moody she is!'" because she could use a little attitude adjustment.

Kids want to be Hollywood perfect. Frankly, we would all prefer to be sensational and flawless, but as parents, we are older and wiser. We realize that even the gloss of perfection hides flaws revealed with just a minimum of peeking under the hood. The most awesome prototype "perfect" car may look strange to others. ("Those headlights have a weird bat-shape.") Some of the imperfections about which kids complain ("I'm too tall.") are very desirable in others. ("I would love to be a girl tall enough to play basketball.") We have things we can change about ourselves (get a haircut) and things we cannot ("My feet are too big but I have great balance.") The inventory is not only endless in quantity but in quality as well. Does your teen accept differences in others or barely tolerate them?

Why don't we explore the "dating dealership." You go to the dealership if you want to sell a car, and you also go to the dealership if you want to buy a car. If you really want to sell, you clean up your vehicle, vacuum out the dog hair and the gum wrappers, spackle the large holes, shine up the chrome. You collect old receipts to prove that your baby has spankin' new tires and five year's worth of semi-monthly oil changes. In short, you put that car's best wheel forward so the dealer can put a price on it.

What you should **NOT** do is drag it in directly from an afternoon of hunting on the muddy trails, hop out of the driver's side in your camo gear, with cans and fast food bags spilling out at the dealer's feet and say, "How much is this baby worth?"

👪 Model It...

When you first get up in the morning, grab your briefcase or purse and pretend to walk out the door with your hair askew, wearing frayed PJ's and morning breath, saying, "I'm going to look for a new job. I'll be back later." See if anyone tackles you and says "Like THAT?!" Ask them how many kids at school see someone in worse shape than that and never say anything. (But, boy, are they thinking it.) Define "Dress for Success" and what that means.

Remember, our kids are on the showroom floor all day at their school. Let's press our noses up to the glass of the dealership windows and take a good look at our precious babies. First impressions count. Are they cleaned up, shiny and ready for show? It's not what (or who) they look like, but their own external "okay-ness" with themselves that matters. Cars have big hoods, kids have big noses. So what? It is their individuality that is important as they create their "brand." Do they like long hair or short? Do they dress up or down? Do they dress like everyone else or step out in their own shoes? ("Ben buttons his shirts up to his chin because he's comfortable that way.") Just because your student doesn't care for a particular style, doesn't mean they have to criticize it. They don't have to buy a car they aren't attracted to and they don't have to date someone they aren't attracted to. But they *do* have to be nice. Help your student understand that all kids go through a period of discovery about who they are and who they want to be.

> ➡ Every student needs to find their own signature, not forge their parent's name.

Kids will tell each other how their look is "working," especially girls. Ever host a roomful of giggling, wired, pre-teen girls doing makeovers on each other? You will need a nap when it's over.

They will critique each other with the perceptive cruelty that only comes from BFF (best friends forever). "Oh Mimi, I love that blush on you! It makes your eyes look as big as Bambi's." "Suzy, that blue lipstick makes you look like Elvis. He's dead, right?" They can be brutally honest with each other, and after the tears wash the mascara away, they may be wearing less make-up and less confidence.

Boys, on the other hand, are generally less concerned about their style. They might grab any old ratty thing from off their floor. Some "fashion-don't" victims just sniff-test an article of clothing and put it on. Guys will rarely criticize each other's fashion choices, although I have overheard them offer the occasional, instantaneous disappointment to one of their group: "Dude. Speedo?" In a sudden burst of self-awareness, your son may decide to take a female friend shopping to boost his fashion morale. When *she* tells him what looks good, it will resonate far more than if you tell him. "Jake, you look totally hot in those jeans," does not have the same impact coming out of his mother's mouth. If his dad says it, it's the kiss of death.

➡ **In school, kids are like a walking, talking car commercial all day long**

Unfortunately, the appearance on the exterior counts tremendously. We agree. But after we get beyond that, then what? Once you look under the hood, what do you see? Those cars in the auto show with the extra-shimmery finish? Ooh, they look hot! But guess what, 90% of them never become real cars. They are just a designer's dream of what a car should look like. You could probably motor it out of the show room, zip through the Burger King drive-thru and get a lot of looks, but a week later the highly specialized engine blows a rod and there are no replacement parts. It becomes a very large, sweet-looking paperweight to keep your credit card bills from blowing away. You just invested a fortune in a glorious ride that cannot go forward.

Is it not the same with people? What are we like under our shiny exteriors? Does your daughter need a new muffler because she announces her presence wherever she travels? "He said WHAT? NO WAY! That's totally AWESOME!!" The entire mall full of people (the ones that aren't deaf) now knows that he's TOTALLY AWESOME. Consider investing in a Dale Carnegie course for her birthday. The value will far outlast a department store gift card.

Does your son belittle and criticize his friends? "Your mom is a jerk." Or is he supportive when they do good things? "Yeah, Vinnie, you da man on that marimba." Maybe your son could benefit from a challenge workshop designed for character building. It is our character underneath the fit and finish that determines whether we drive in a straight path. Yes, by all means, you can advertise yourself as a Corvette, but then you better maintain that V-8 engine and keep all the pistons firing. Otherwise you're just a shiny, empty cut-out.

Model It...

Do a thorough examination of the levels of intolerance, judging, bullying, and name calling in your teen. If you see evidence of any negative behavior or verbiage, try this approach:

Tell them about a time when you got cut off by someone on the freeway. Verbalize (within reason) any disapproving thoughts that went through your head about the person. Now imagine that you followed them home and pulled into their driveway only to find out that they were driving absentmindedly because they just got a call that they were fired. Or that their child had been rushed to the hospital. What if they were having a diabetic reaction and couldn't drive straight? How would this change the perspective?

If your teen is overly negative, there are hundreds of acceptance workshops, seminars, character building games and even camps that you might consider. Don't dismiss the signs. Negativity, anger, and aggression are roads you don't want to go down. Look for help.

Okay, we've examined our own kids, now let's shuffle our feet with them out onto the lot and find a model that *they* like. If they veer off in a completely different direction from you, welcome to reality parenting. They don't like our cars. ("A minivan? You want me to drive dad's green *minivan*? Just laugh at me now and save my friends the trouble.") They don't like our clothes. ("Mom, what's with the track suit and bathrobe?") They don't like our choices when it comes to their friends. ("Please don't make me go to the prom with little Willy Gates!") But we know things they don't. A minivan makes sense when you chauffeur six kids and a week's worth of groceries. That bathrobe matches your chauffeur hat. It is comfy and quick to locate when you leap into that ugly minivan at the crack of dawn. Willy Gates grows up to be Bill.

> ➲ **Grandmothers don't usually buy Monster Trucks.**

It seems so obvious to us as parents. Every kid might want to drive a 67' Camaro, but does it make sense? Can they possibly afford it? I hope they never have to transport more than one soccer team at a time. Maybe every high school boy wants to date Tiffany, the head cheerleader, but does that make sense either? He might not be able to afford her taste. The shiniest, the prettiest, the one with the most detailing is not necessarily the one you want to own.

We have to encourage our teens to look beyond the surface finish of other teens and find out what's underneath. If you want to see how a car is made, go to the assembly plant. If you want to see how a person is made, go hang out with their family. Spend an afternoon with your potential in-laws for a snapshot of the manufacturing plant they came from. ("Oh, Sara, how sweet that your mom is a mud wrestler at the Pink Lady Casino. It was so much fun to see her in action! Do you think you will wrestle too?")

German cars are different from Japanese cars. Cadillac makes the Escalade. Each brand says something about the quality, the strengths, and the weaknesses of its products. In the same way, every student is a product of his or her own environment. They have been molded, manufactured, parented in a way specific to their family. How much research have you put into your car design and assembly specs? Would it not be worth it to visit the family where your son's girlfriend was "assembled"?

Of course you can't schedule a tour of their house, but you can stop by, actually walk up to the door, and say "Hello." You will probably have several opportunities to pick up and drop off (remember, you are the master chauffeur). Just go on up to the door with your student when you pick up their date. Say, "Hi, I'm Fred, the overworked, underpaid father of Nina. I just wanted to introduce myself..." A little volley of small talk can tell you so much about the parents' attitude and demeanor. When you go to the door you might say, "I'm Carol. Thank you for having my son Max over. Here are some cookies for the kids." It is good to get a visual. If a big angry dad waddles to the door and yells, "Who's interrupting my game?!" why, that tells you just a little something about that family. On the other hand, if the mom comes to the door, overwhelmed but pleasant none-the-less, greets you with a smile and says, "Oh, I'm so glad you came to the door and introduced yourself. Thank you," then you know she's "good people."

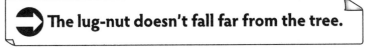

The lug-nut doesn't fall far from the tree.

If your students are driving themselves to these "dates," you can still call the parents ahead of time, introduce yourself, confirm the plans, and ask if your teen should bring something. Chips and salsa? Pink lemonade? A "PG" movie for the kids to watch?

Would you ever consider buying a car without looking under the hood, without test driving it, without finding out what this button does? Our kids date this way. They look at the visual appeal of the metallic sparkle and decide to buy, buy, buy before they try, try, try! A kid might fall in love over a favorite cologne. I mean, who doesn't love that new car smell? We should teach our children to use all of their senses when choosing any relationship but more importantly, use all their *sense*.

The more time you spend driving a particular car, the more familiar you become with its habits and handling. The more hours your child logs with a particular person before any serious commitment, the easier it is to walk away financially, emotionally, and physically if necessary. Look under the hood. Test drive it. Check out the dealership. Meet the parents. Converse with this potential new beau.

When your student buys his first car, you want him to do a little research. There are no perfect cars. They are all flawed in some way. Even a Maserati can blow a gasket. There are no perfect humans. We are all flawed; we can all blow a gasket. Real people do not resemble Brad and Angelina. Most of us look more like Larry the Cable Guy. But even Larry is kind of cute when he puts on his freshly laundered flannel shirt. It is important for our teens to remember not to compare themselves to a Cosmo cover. Choose your own style, brush your teeth, wash your hair, put on a clean shirt. Your first impression matters, but let it be an impression of **YOU** and not a gorgeous paint job with gerbils running a wheel for an engine.

🏠 Drive It Home...

DIA-LOG with your student by asking these questions...

I actually used YouTube™ for this: find a video of a car being assembled. For more realistic drama, take your child to an auto manufacturing plant where they assemble the cars. Here's the picture: your student wants a new car. They have been fantasizing about it for months. They know exactly what they want. Finally you agree to let them have it because they just turned 16. The problem is they were so impatient that they went to the factory and got the car off the assembly line before it was finished. It was only a freshly painted, flawless body with nothing inside... just the shell. A few days later, your child is devastated because "it never went anywhere". There was never even a chance.

Not all teens are "put together" by sixteen. Discuss how relationships can fail because there are pieces missing. If a part like maturity, independence, or wisdom is missing, how far can the relationship go? Define what it would mean to be a fully assembled, complete person so your student can navigate these difficult turns. If we can encourage them to slow down and really pay attention to what drives relationships, they will have a better chance of completing the course.

Parents, complete the following questions and discuss with your student:

What kind of car do you currently drive? _____

What does your car say about you? _____

What kind of car would your child choose? _____

What does that say about them? _____

OK parents. How would you have answered these questions as a teenager? Do you answer differently today? Can we expect our kids to know what they will want 20 years from now? Is it realistic for your student to think they have it figured out?

Have your student say the very first word that comes to mind for each of the brands below.

Honda _____

Dodge _____

BMW _____

Jaguar _____

Saturn _____

Have your student name the top five things they want in a car. Have them name the car of their dreams:

1. _____

2. _____

3. _____

4. _____

5. _____

Dream car: Year _____ Make _____ Model _____

Now do the same with a relationship. Ask your student to describe the top five qualities they are looking for in the ideal boyfriend or girlfriend.

1. _____

2. _____

3. _____

4. _____

5. _____

🚐 Test Drive...

Student:
Exterior. At the dealership, a window sticker lists the specifics of the vehicle. Look in the mirror and check out your exterior "window sticker" reflection:

Hygiene — generally clean, smell good, clean hands and fingernails
Hair — clean and brushed, compliments who you are. (Is it purple because you like it?)
Teeth — brushed, clean, fresh breath
Smile — look approachable, happy, easy to be around
Dress — your personal best, clean clothes, compliments your style, flatters you
Overall Appearance — care about the way you look
Other _____
Other _____

What does your branding say about you?

> ➡ **Mirrors were invented to check ourselves, not others.**

Interior. Under the hood. Outward appearance is only part of the picture. Check out your interior "window sticker" to identify your brand and condition.

This model comes standard with:

Mood—energetic, fun, easy going, positive attitude, nice, polite, respectful of others

Judgment—good choices, good priorities, work hard for grades, doesn't drink, smoke or do drugs, good moral compass, headed in a good, general direction

Friend—good listener, caring, other-centered, understanding, good advice, helpful

Character—loyal, honest, doesn't gossip, faithful, humble, good boundaries, trustworthy

Financial Sense—has a job, spends wisely, generous with others

Family—values, respect, healthy perspective

Spiritual—sound perspective on faith, does not judge others for their beliefs

History—corrected past mistakes, no major overhaul needed, very few wrecks

More options included (what is your uniqueness):

Other _____

Other _____

I am a: (brand) _____ (model) _____ (year) _____

Read Your Manual!

~

"No man is worth your tears, but once you've found one that is, he won't make you cry."

—Mae West

When buying a used car, punch the buttons on the radio. If all the stations are rock and roll, there's a good chance the transmission is shot."

—Larry Lujack

"Women with "pasts" interest men because men hope history will repeat itself."

—Mae West

"Men are all alike — except the one you've met who's different."

—Mae West

8 Salesmen or Pit Crew?

I had worn out the old Satellite. I was tired of driving that humiliating Army-green barge on wheels and wanted something cute and smart to compliment my "educated college girl" look. My dad drove me to a dealership owned by a friend of his. After eliminating everything I could not afford, I proudly signed on the dotted line to buy an adorable Plymouth Horizon. It was the perfect reflection of me: sassy, cute, fun, and smart. It was robin's egg blue, had a sunroof and an 8-track player. I had arrived.

I was giddy with how impressed my friends would be. My dad said congratulations and left in his own car. I got behind the wheel and smiled as wide as Montana at the half a dozen salesmen waving me off on my maiden voyage. I turned the key and hit the accelerator. The car lurched forward and died. It happened so fast, there was no time to hide. Manual… not automatic. Did I miss something?

I had no idea how to drive a stick. So much for that smart, sassy look I was aiming for. I spent the next hour taking lessons in the dealership parking lot so I could drive it home without stalling and stuttering. Headline: "College Girl Utterly Humiliated by Smart, Sassy Blue Horizon." What had happened? I had let the experts, my dad and his friend the car salesman, make my purchasing decisions for me. The emotional high of having a new car smothered my logic. I was so wrapped up in how cute it was, I completely missed the fact that I was not prepared for the car I was buying.

How many teens are in relationships beyond their adolescent capabilities? ("Julie is so lucky! She is dating a college senior named "Animal" and she is only 15.") Kids are jolted, misled by their chemistry, and cannot control their cooling systems. Too much horsepower overwhelms their underdeveloped control modules. This is not to imply that young people are in any way stupid. Absolutely not. To whom else would you turn to program your thermostat or solve a Rubik's cube? The point is, they can become awfully distracted by the pretty colors and veer into oncoming traffic while following a beautiful set of taillights.

They rarely travel alone, these young people. They ride in herds, traffic jams of kids, giving each other advice, "supporting" each other, selling each other the goods all around them. ("You are awesome at Guitar Hero. My boyfriend has a cousin who can nail Motley Crue on expert level, and he's only been playing for the two months since he got out of jail. You should go out with him. We could all hang together.")

Your student is surrounded by people daily who are eager to sell them something. There is no shortage of teenagers who will step right into the roll of "Car Salesman" and advise your student on the perfect ride. The trouble is, like some real car salesmen, these experts may not have your child's best interests in mind. If you are a hungry buyer, and you think you want to own a Corvette, you will find yourself a salesman who will sell you a Corvette. You don't pull into "Al's Slightly Dusty Subaru" lot. You don't want Al's reliable automobile, you don't want to hear Al tell you about how safe and fuel-efficient his cars are, even if it's the affordable way to drive to work every day. No, you want to find Slick Rick at "Hot Rod Adventures" to put you in a metallic red, turbo-charged beast. It's not Slick Rick's job to sell you the insurance, just to get you behind the wheel.

So who sells to our kids? Who are the car salesmen in our kid's lives? (Note: the word "salesmen" is intended to be gender non-specific. I am fully aware that there are great Car Saleswomen and Car Salespeople. "Salesmen" is just so much easier to say. Please don't be offended. My brother sells cars and I love him!) Most often, the salesmen will be our kids' schoolmates. This is not so horrible when it comes to, say, shoe advice. ("Buy some flip flops. Who cares if they're bad for your posture, they're so cute with your green toenail polish!") But when it comes to matchmaking, their friends can fail in a number of categories.

The friends are inexperienced. ("Shelby, you are gonna LOVE this guy. He wears a blue hoodie just like you!") They don't always have your best interests in mind. ("Shelby, he's got a really hot car and he can drive ALL of us to the mall. His dad has a lawyer friend that got his points taken off from the DUI.") They are only salesmen; they are not the ones who have to drive the vehicle. Whatever happens to you after your "purchase" does not impact them. Look closely at their motivation. Some salesmen are just careless, but some can be downright self-serving. ("Don't blame me that he actually had a pregnant girlfriend. I only told you he was cute.")

So what are we to do, as the parents of these impressionable children? Yes, the "salesman" with the poor recommendation might feel a bit guilty as your student crashes into misery, but it's your student who does the driving. It is your daughter who will cry at night after Lance Romance cheats on her. It is your son who will mope and fail math when the GF dumps him for being too nice, the same way she ended the last seven relationships. Your student will be the one that has to write the break up letter, not you, and certainly not their trusted "experts."

> **Who pays for the broken fuel pump in your student's car? The car your best friend talked them into buying?**

What we can do is teach our kids about taking more ownership in their decisions so they are not as vulnerable. But how? Kids are still not experienced in the ways of the world, are they? No, especially when it comes to revealing the reality behind a pretty face. ("But what else do you need to know, Rachel? Look at his smile!") For one thing, our kids need to be armed with knowledge. We can guide our kids to find the information out for themselves, and then let's be honest here, follow that up with our own research. ("After all, his pretty smile sits right under that dagger tattoo below his left eye. What else do you need to know, Rachel?")

If your son wants to buy a car, he can read Consumer Reports to find out what they say about the safety tests, frequency of repairs, cost, and fuel efficiency for a particular car. CR will flat-out tell you what models to avoid and what models are recommended. Perhaps your daughter wants to buy the little Honda she saw for sale in the front yard of a farmhouse. She could pull up a CARFAX vehicle history report to tell her if the car has ever been wrecked or flooded. Use the information you have to investigate what you might be buying.

If your student is not yet interested in all the techno-temptations, by all means, **DO NOT STEER THEM THERE!** MySpace™, Facebook™, IM's, Texting and the Internet will all be there when your student is ready to roll. If, however, the momentum is already building towards that end, I would highly recommend using the technology that is available to your advantage. Your kids certainly will. Sure, you could ban your daughter from having a MySpace™ account, but she is capable of creating one anyway at her friend's house. I can name three kids today that have accounts under different names that their parents know nothing about. Instead of being so fearful of it, use it. Share a MySpace™ account with your student or even build your own. (Your child will show you how.) You are entitled to have the password for all accounts at all times. (You can do this. They are still underage and dependent on you. Be strong, brave buffalo.) Then, look at it. Look people up. With your teen sitting right there with you.

"So, sweetie, your friend Ashlee says that Jonathan is a nice boy who would never say a harsh word about anybody. Let's look at his MySpace™ page. Huh. It says right here, now tell me if I'm translating this wrong, 'I hate that @!#*&% science teacher. She's a B@*!ch and I'm not doing her homework anymore.' So what exactly did Ashlee base her assessment on? I'll bet he has pretty eyes."

Model It...

Spend some time on MySpace™ or Facebook™ becoming familiar with the latest virtual hangouts. Browse for some examples to share with your student. (Keep track of the links). Learn how to read the profile pages and what to look for so when the time comes, you can "browse" with your student. Have enough of both good and bad examples to choose from and use them as teaching tools.

+ I highly recommend that parental controls be enabled at all times. Log students on only when you are there and only temporarily in case you forget that you disabled the security.

Salesmen don't always tell you everything. They might only tell you just enough to get you to buy the car. They put the cars they need to sell out front, and put the best deals at the back of the lot. They might neglect to inform you that the last three models of this car were recalled, that it drives like a steamboat, or that "your mileage may vary." Vary a lot. They want to sell you the car because they need the paycheck. This is not a bad motivation, but as always, "Buyer Beware." You simply must investigate on your own. Test-drive it. Look up what other people have said about its reliability. Get the word-of-mouth opinion – from people you trust. Look beyond the tri-fold brochure on the desk. After all, if your "friend" steers you toward a "loser" guy, it just might be because she wants the "winner" for herself. Examine the motivation behind all your salesmen. You don't walk onto the lot and buy the first convertible car you see. Jumping into the first relationship you see because she has solid struts is just hormonal thinking. Control your chassis there, fella.

Everybody has advice to give, wanted or unwanted, some good, and some bad, some of it entirely inappropriate for your child. ("Oh, Tim is so handsome and he has such a good job at the country club parking cars. I'm sure he only sleeps around because he hasn't found the right girl yet.") To whom should your child listen? Let's switch gears. Instead of trying to find that one perfect salesman, what if our children were surrounded by folks who genuinely "have their back"? What if they assembled a pit crew of skilled experts with a keen eye and goals similar to their own?

Indy 500 racers are strapped into the driver's seat by their team, a team of racing experts. The pit crew's job is to keep the car safe, accident-free, and of course, to win. The driver stays in constant contact with his crew. Each member is hand-picked, highly-trained, and trustworthy. It is in all of their best interests that the driver does not crash. (No driver, no job.) The crew has an entirely different perspective from the driver. They can see what the driver cannot. ("Breaker, breaker, good buddy, your wheel's on fire.") They can see cars rolling end over end around the next curve. They know when you can put the pedal down because it's clean clear to Flag Town. They know how you have run before ("Too close to the wall, Joe!") and they know what is coming up behind you ("Here comes that pretty blonde thing with nothing on her mind but leaving you in the dust.")

Kids need the reliable and continuous influx of information that their pit crew relays to them. Your student speeds around the track on an adrenaline rush, no mirrors, falling in love with every little chassis that shimmies, they need some self-less, not self-centered, people to be their ears, their eyes, even their wisdom. ("Hey, Mia, you have tried to overtake this little Sports Car six times. It ain't working, sweetheart. Decelerate and back off. He looks down his spoiler at you.")

> ➡ **The time to pick your pit crew is before the race has started.**

The pit crew needs to be assembled long before the start of the race, long before you hear: "Gentlemen, start your engines." Every aspect of racing is discussed and diagrammed before you speed down the stretch toward the checkered flag. Safety is of utmost importance. They constantly keep an eye out for upcoming road hazards so you don't have a blow-out before the race is over. ("Hey, Alex, you fell asleep in math class today. What gives?") The driver's ability is constantly monitored. ("You know, Samantha, I've seen your reaction to that smile before. You hit the wall last time. His sparkling grill shouldn't throw you off again.") The pit crew is aware that safety is vital, that upcoming road hazards need to be communicated quickly. Failure to do so can devastate a team. ("Perfume spill at the second turn! Veer left!")

Your student might not be able to pick a pit crew by him or herself. After all, these are the same kids who let someone convince them to skip school after lunch. As manager, owner, and rescuer of the driver, you (the parent) may need to assist them with these Human Resource issues. ("So who sold you on the idea to wear a bikini top and a shawl to church? I'd like to have a talk with this Sunflower Patchouli.")

Model It...

Write a blank check for $10,000 and hand it to your teen.

Read out loud to your student: **THIS IS AN EXERCISE and NO, YOU CANNOT HAVE THE CHECK WHEN WE ARE DONE.** (Silly kids.)

Tell your student: I am going to write 10 names on the "Pay to the order of" line on this check. These 10 people

together will use this check to buy you a car. You will not be able to speak to these 10 people about what you want before they buy the car. Think carefully — who are those 10 people?

Your student's answer to this exercise gives you a good starting point for who should be in their "pit crew."

If your student doesn't have 10 friends for their Pit Crew, start with five. These should be the kids they see every day... and trust every day. These should be the people they "do" life with. If your student is having trouble coming up with a list of their own, this might be a great time to recommend kids you know that they hadn't thought of. Have your student invite these other teens to be in their Pit Crew, meaning that they are willing to make sound observations and tell the truth about what they see.

Now that your teen has sifted out a top-notch pit crew from the self-interested salesmen around her, she still wants to shop. We need to remind our little darlings that most of the inventory on the showroom floor should really be in the used car lot. There may be some fully ripe "lemons" on the lot but regardless, all these kids have some mileage on them. Even the shyest, most studious kid in physics class has been living and creating a history for himself. It is imperative that our kids take a look at the sticker on the window and find out what roads every potential date has traveled before. CARFAX would tell you if a vehicle has been ridden hard and used as a taxi cab. Consumer Reports will tell you that a particular model blows a tie rod when more than four crash dummies take it for a joy ride. So which model should humans carpool in?

> ➲ **Nothing in the "dating dealership" has zero miles on it.**

Consider the ancient form of communication: no, not smoke signals, talking to people. ("You mean in person? No electricity required?") You can do this. People are still a great source of stories and insight despite their overwhelming need to be attached to their cell phones. Ok, fine, go ahead and call.

Model it...

- Ask for three to five adult references to inquire about someone your child is going to date. Get phone numbers and actually make the calls.

- Check with teachers, friends, neighbors, pastors that you trust to give any pertinent information.

- Meet the parents at least by phone, but preferably in person.

And by all means let us not forget this great age of information. This is the age of YouTube™ and MySpace™. By the time this book is published, we'll probably wear holograms of our complete history hidden somewhere under our left earlobe. You want to know what I did in 1978? Just press this button on my neck. (And then please let *me* know because it was all a blur.) But for now let's use the technology we have. Look someone up. Google their name. ("Well, what have we here? I thought you said Mara doesn't drink, but she has a video of herself on YouTube™ doing a keg-stand with a skirt on. That's odd.")

You can easily discover important information about a person, frequently because they advertise their own crazy behavior. Read a person's blog. They publish them on the web for someone to read, why not you? A student's blog tends to be a candid advertisement either in their favor or against it. Look at their MySpace™ page. Is it covered with nasty photos of binge drinking? Dripping skulls and gas masks? Pentagrams? Explore these with your teen sitting right beside you. It's one thing to describe a car wreck. It's another, much more vivid, experience to witness the carnage together.

Yes, these kids are young. They are trying to "find themselves." Most are not yet fully assembled individuals who experiment a little with this strange style and that passing interest, and it may be years before they actually land in a "final" personality. (Did anyone else go to high school with the guy who only wore a long black coat and mumbled but who is now a successful animator?) Even though kids have a history, they are not who they are likely to become in real life. We need to teach our kids not to judge too harshly or too quickly, but to maintain a healthy caution about others' behavior. Not every strange behavior is a red flag. Just because Johnny doesn't wash his hair every day, doesn't necessarily mean that he's indifferent or unaware. Maybe his family is struggling financially.

And yes, many, even most of these kids have a ton of unrealized potential. The trick is to teach your student to sift through the sticker features to find what works. A car with potential might not go anywhere without a complete overhaul. An investment in a relationship must be examined in the same way. Unfortunately, some kids have already exhibited behaviors that render their "value" as a potential date sliding downhill fast. ("Dad, Nathan has only been suspended twice for his temper. He's just mad because he hates school. This summer he will be so much cooler.") How much of an investment does your child want to make overhauling their new date to prove out his potential? Would you want them spending all their time and money trying to restore a car that was in a six-car pile up?

No kid is freshly made; no teenager was freshly formed and baked just this morning with the freshness seal. You have to ask around. You have to look around. You have to talk around with your friends, on the web, to other parents, to coaches, to the local cops if necessary to find out about this prince who is taking your princess to the prom. Make sure that your precious teen is surrounded by a skilled and focused pit crew and not a self-serving cluster of grinning salesmen. The lemon law says that you can return a bad car. It does not apply to bad dates.

🏠 Drive It Home...

DIA-LOG with your student by asking these questions...

Identifying "Red Flags"

Read these data points with your student. Discuss whether they are or are not "red flags." Is everything as it appears? Is there a need to gather more information? How could your student expand his understanding of the facts?

- Your math teacher warns you to be careful sitting next to Sean
- Emily's sister is going to repeat 7th grade
- Tina wants to be an exchange student
- Joe is joining the military right after high school
- Amanda says she has a job offer after graduation as a full time model
- Nathan is good enough to make the Olympics next year in gymnastics
- Beth is probably not going to graduate

Buying a car? Get some facts. How many miles are on it? What is the history and current condition? Was it built to last? Is it dependable? Is it safe?

Looking ahead is not a common trait for teens. Encouraging them to get beyond immediate gratification is challenging but critical to improving their dating habits.

🚐 Test Drive...

Student:
Going on a date? Ask questions. Who is going to help you sort through the maze on the lot? Assemble a dependable pit crew who will hold you accountable and keep you safe.

Do some research. Knowing the "DATEFAX" can save you a lot of emotional turmoil. Let's break these facts down into three categories:

History — What has happened so far?
I'm selling my car. If I smoked in it, never changed the oil filter, and hit a deer, would you buy it? _____

What if I sprayed some air freshener and never mentioned the lack of oil changes or the deer? It's the same car. Now would you buy it? _____

Reminder to parents: students should gather data before they buy. Encourage them to use their pit crew for a clearer perspective.

Identifying "Red Flags"
Decide which of these are red flags and why:

- Sara has had six boyfriends in four months
- Bethany has never had a boyfriend because it is not her top priority
- Max has been suspended from school twice
- Katie has missed several days of school this year
- Justin just got fired from his job
- There are rumors about what Amy did at the Homecoming dance
- Michael has lived in 7 different places

Present Condition — What is it like right now?
If a driver wrecks his car, pays to have it fixed, and then keeps driving out of control, would you ride with them?

_____

If you fall in love with a car that is rusted out, needs a front-end alignment, and is on the top-ten list for "most unreliable," would you buy the car? _____

Everyone makes mistakes but not everyone learns from them. There are many reasons why a student might still part of the "available" inventory. Is it by choice?

Identifying "Red Flags"
Decide which of these are red flags and why. Give three possible scenarios for each:

- Allison wears extremely revealing clothes and looks hot
- Greg washes his hair three out of seven days
- Deena flirts with your best friend
- Trevor has a job at a gas station
- Cody never smiles
- Heather does not live with her parents

Future Promise — What will it be like tomorrow?
"Consumer Reports" says the car you are buying will lose over half of its value in one year. Do you buy it anyway?

_____

You found a car that is everything you were looking for but is number one on the manufacturers' recall list. Is this a good investment? _____

On a piece of paper, write who your best friend was in first grade, second grade, third grade… up to today.

Choose any one of those old names and answer the following question: Would share your deepest darkest secret today with that former BFF? _____

Given the usual length of "best friend forever," do you trust your current "best friend" to give you advice knowing the consequences of that advice might last longer than the friendship itself? _____

In the blanks below, write in the names of your top five closest friends that you are currently doing life with. When it comes to advice, are they a Car Salesman or part of your Pit Crew?

_____ Car Salesman or Pit Crew

_____ Car Salesman or Pit Crew

_____ Car Salesman or Pit Crew

_____ Car Salesman or Pit Crew

_____ Car Salesman or Pit Crew

Read Your Manual!

This little piggy went to market… to buy a car. What were the other four little piggies doing?

Don't you think it would be a good idea to ask the other little piggies what they thought about the car before you put down the deposit? If you make an unwise choice, don't come running "wee, wee, wee, wee… all the way home!"

~

"You'll learn more about
a road by traveling it
than by consulting all
the maps in the world."

~ Author Unknown

Start Your Engines!

Rush hour in San Diego, California is not a bad place when you have a convertible, and I did. She was a beauty: a white Mustang with red leather interior. The leather required constant maintenance and the car guzzled gas like a fighter jet, but I didn't care. I looked good sitting in that baby. I was hot. (So I thought.)

One perfect California day, a warm Santa Anna breeze was whipping the salt sea air around my tangled blonde hair, and I was zipping up the I-5 to see some friends. Huey Lewis was blaring on the radio, the top was down, it was perfect. I had a casual arm resting on the door and a huge smile as a bus load of adolescent soccer boys pulled up next to me blowing kisses. Just as I turned to wave "Hi boys!" a flock of seagulls dumped nine yards of seagull poop all over my gorgeous self. These kamikaze sky rats bombed up my arm, across my chest, splatted my hot new Ray Bans, and as a final insult, they dropped a load on my wind-whipped hair. I had left the house in my dream car; I was now driving in a nightmare.

Book smarts don't make you a good driver, nor do they make you a good dater. The first part of this book has been a parallel to the classroom hours of Driver's Ed — you learn some of the rules of the road, what the parts of the car do, how to shop the used car lot, but now you have to actually start the engine and use what you've learned.

So here we go. This is the moment we've all been waiting for. Get in and drive. You're about to take off on your first practice run. Let's do a quick safety check. Have you done the prep work? Let's review:

Good sense vs. good *senses* check. Let's agree that we're all human, even teenagers, and that we can't help but be attracted to pretty things. (For some, that represents the entire realm of their dating criteria: "Ooh, she's so sparkly! I want that one!")

Acknowledging the fact that looks count means two things for our intrepid daters:

1. Clean up your quarter panels. Shine up the grill. Take a shower, change your shirt, check your teeth for broccoli bits. Mint up your breath. Listerine only burns for a minute. Fix your hair. (Allow an extra 45 minutes for this, just in case.) Make your best outward appearance. It mattered to you when you were picking and choosing. It matters just as much to them that you don't smell like the fry bin at Wendy's.

2. Having said all that, remember that building a relationship on outward appearance is not enough. That silver Auto Show prototype might look gorgeous under the spotlights, but you have no idea how well it handles until you actually drive it through your neighborhood. Girls with too much makeup aren't real good in the pool. Guys with Mohawks are not very popular when you have to sit behind them in the theatre. Things look different when you put them in motion.

➡ **Has your dating sense been overruled by your senses?**

Money check. There are certainly some free activities in this world, but few teens I've met clamor for those. No, most young people want to do things that cost somebody something. What arrangements have we made with our teens? Who's buying, Daddy Deep Pockets or Unfortunate Son? Please re-read *Chapter 6 — "Qualifying for Dater's Ed"* for some suggestions on how to keep it fair. And don't forget "hidden" costs like dating clothes, gas money, and cash for tips. In *Chapter 11 — "Boundary Lines"* we will explore the spending limits. (A word here: teach your teenagers to never, ever skimp on tipping their food server. No matter how closely they are counting their change at the end of the night, always tip the wait staff 20%. And round up. If you can't do the math, you can't date. Tipping generously not only looks good, it's the right thing to do.)

Background check. We've already talked about "asking around," about running a DATEFAX on your potential dates. We saw in *Chapter 8 — "Salesmen or Pit Crew"* that it is important to check out who our babies are going to hang with, consulting their own, self-published advertising campaigns (MySpace™, Facebook™, Google™). This is no joke. Let me tell you a true story of an exciting young man who waltzed into our little world and nearly wreaked some serious havoc in the lives of some treasured young women. Fortunately, a little background check revealed his shocking and dangerous history. I'll call him "Rich." Rich was introduced to my daughter at a birthday party. Average looks, slightly older, polite and seemingly quite nice. He reappeared online a year later from another state where he was currently living and was casually pursuing my daughter. So I started to ask around. And here's where it gets interesting. Nobody would have said anything about this guy until I asked. That is when I heard through a client, a friend, another mom, and even the police (yes, the cops!) that he was more than just trouble. Can you say drug-dealing flasher who dropped out of high school with a police record? The information was there the whole time, just for the asking. Here is the good news and the bad news: The entire crisis developed and was quashed in less than five days. It was over in a matter of minutes because I did the research. Do your homework and follow your gut. It's worth it.

 **Model it...**

> Show your teen the reality of how close pedophiles and sex offenders live by doing an online search. By entering your address, you can see the actual names of those offenders, pictures, and even where they live. Be sure to do the same search near their school as well. Make certain your students are well aware how close to home this serious issue lurks. This is not a recommendation for girls only.

Now that you've done your safety check, it's time to start logging some hours. You might ask, "What's it all for?" "What exactly am I doing here?" You're not alone. Philosophers much deeper than you or me have been asking that since before The Flood. We will only try to answer "what are we doing here" as it relates to the first date.

It is highly unlikely that the "first date ever" will lead to marriage, however there is that slim, remote chance. It is unlikely that you will see this same new, young couple 50 years from now in a two-seater rocking chair recalling how it first began: "You know, Clarence, we've been together, what, 50 years? And it all started with that dating book by that red-headed convertible driver, what was her name? Oh yeah, "Mama J." Smart gal, that Lisa Jander. Clarence! I'm over here, Clarence." But... stranger things have happened.

Don't panic. The goal of their first time seeing each other is very simple: to get to know one another. It is not to see a movie. It is not to eat a cheeseburger. It is not to just sit on the couch. You can do all those things with your grandma. A practice "date" is just a way for you to learn what is inside this hot new honey that looked so good to you in the lunch line.

Model it...

At the car dealership, you need to tell the Salesperson whether you are interested in either "Leasing" or "Buying." You don't let them choose for you. This is a very important dating skill that your student will find useful again and again; I call it the "Lease Agreement." Speed dating is not what we are after here. Slowing things down takes proficiency and practice, and one of the keys to not being caught off guard is to be prepared for an obvious offer that is likely to come your student's way.

If your student is presented with an "Offer to Purchase" on the third date, how will they respond? Try this: "I really like hanging out with you. I don't know you well enough to be your BF or GF, but maybe we can spend more time together and get to know each other." Have your student change the language to fit their own speaking style and practice it so it rolls off their tongue.

So, how do you get to know this other student? The single, number one, all-time best way to get to know somebody is, hold on to your hats, this is big: *talk to them*. And guess what, there are right ways and wrong ways to do this. (Of course there are. Why else would we write books about it?)

There is real conversation, and there is small talk. There is nothing wrong with small talk. This is talk about obvious, usually meaningless things about which any two strangers might converse. "Sure looks like rain." "Yup." "Did you see the Lions game on Sunday?" "Yeah, that Rocket McOverpaid sure has an arm on him." Of course, small talk may not tell you very much about your date unless they respond with: "Rain? You call this rain? This ain't nothing. Why once I conjured up a rain storm so fierce that dogs took to howling my name." If your date says this, run immediately home.

Then there is real conversation. Real conversation is the back-and-forth exchange of verbal information between two people. *This* is the point of logging hours with that certain special someone. You are flying high, buzzing around the hallways because you are so attracted to this hot chickie who said hello to you in band. Let's keep all four tires on the road and find out if there's anything under the hood first. You have to log some quality hours with this person before you can know if this is really worth pursuing.

> **If you don't know where you're going… any road will do.**

Let's talk a little more about logging hours. I mentioned in a previous chapter that a student dater needs to log hours with his or her potential date. The point of logging hours in driving is to, yes, that's right, gain some *experience* driving. And just like driving, a student dater needs to log hours dating before he, again you are correct, gains some experience in getting to know this other person. Are they "officially" dating or driving? Not really. They are learning and practicing.

When your student first begins logging driving hours, they will be focused so much on just keeping the car between the two white lines, that they will miss other important signs along the road that give them clues about what lies further on down the road. In their first 10 hours of driving, all they can see is the windshield, some dotted lines, and a new color called "Sheer Terror." The more they drive, the more they will notice the bigger picture. They can begin to anticipate what a driver in front of them might do. They can look ahead and see the traffic conditions and adjust accordingly.

The same is true in dating. In the beginning they're just trying not to crash. They're just trying to be wonderful or at least likeable. But as time goes on and they log more hours with an individual, the drive changes — the view changes. They can focus beyond the straightaway and they can begin to anticipate certain behaviors. Your student can see signs of things to come. The level of intensity increases and the subtle details become clearer. "You know what? That white Pontiac is weaving all over the road up there. I think I'll change lanes and avoid him." That's not something your student might notice while they are first learning to drive, but they will as they log hours. "You know, Nate has kicked his dog the last three Sundays in a row. I think I will avoid him." See? They are starting to notice things as they spend time with their date.

"Why do I have to do this?" your kid might ask. "Can't we just hang out?" No. Because by logging hours you are proving to me, the parent, that you are *intentionally* trying to learn something more important about this person *other* than the fact that they look good in jeans. There is evidence that you're not on cruise control, but that you are actively learning about the pros and the cons in this relationship. In your first 10 hours of dating you might only notice things like "Mmm… he smells good." But after the first 20 hours you begin to notice more subtle things, like perhaps he has a fetish for raising boa constrictors and you hate snakes. Or good things: that he's truly a gentle soul and this relationship is worth investing another 30 hours in.

 **Not all dates come "fully loaded."**

Requiring your student to log dating hours proves to you (and to themselves) that they have done the personal research required to make a commitment to actually be "seeing" this "boyfriend" or "girlfriend." You may want to require a minimum like Driver's Ed does, create an agreement between you (the State) and your teen (the driver/dater). Here would be an example of a "Dating Permit": Your student must log 60 worthwhile dating hours getting to know the other student, five of which are in your presence. (Hey now! This is easy compared to the eighteen months they will have to endure with you in the passenger's seat while they learn to drive.)

After two students spend 60 hours getting to know each other and you have had ample dialogue with your teen, you will extend the privilege to let them continue dating on their own. (We know that as parents we will never actually stop worrying, but like in driving, at some point we have to agree to turn over the keys.) My daughter said that this method saved her "from lots of bad dates already!"

And here are the guidelines about these logged hours:

Talk Time: "You have to be able to converse with your date during any given logged hour." A movie doesn't count. Sitting for an hour and a half in front of *"Die Hard 7: Bunions and Broken Glass"* does not qualify as "getting to know you" time. In fact, it might be subtracted from your total due to questionable judgment.

My Time: At least five of these hours must be with me, the parent. That's right. You must bring little Savannah over to meet your dreadful mother and father. We have instincts and perceptions you have not fathomed. (Remember that time I knew you were lighting fires behind the shed and you were astonished that you were caught?) We know things.

Good Time: As a parent, I expect that these hours must be "intentional." I will ask you questions about your date. The questions will likely begin with "Well, what did you learn this time?" You might as well get used to answering in full sentences. Grunts and shrugs are not acceptable, and you'll just have to repeat the class.

Down Time: "If you abuse the privilege, I will take away your keys." Like it or not, the parent is still in charge. Privileges can and will be revoked if your teen pushes the limits of his or her freedoms. There are no shortcuts to being a good driver. You must simply drive in all kinds of weather under a variety of conditions. There is no shortcut to knowing someone well. You cannot possibly know if you two are compatible without spending time together in a variety of conditions.

So how does your teen fulfill the requirements of these logged hours? How does he or she accommodate your request for "intentional" time spent together? Two crucial things:

Dates should be planned in advance.
Here's an example of a poor first road test: Let's suppose this is the day your teen has been waiting for. She has spent hours primping and poofing. Every hair is in place and every eyelash is curled. Soon prince charming will gallop in on his healthy steed and sweep his princess into his arms. They will ride off into the sunset and... (Ding dong.)... "Dad!!!" your princess shouts, forgetting her delicate inside voice in all her excitement. "Get the door! He's here!" Your daughter's dream world is jolted when you open the door to face a scruffy kid wearing ripped jeans and a skull and cross bones T-shirt. A noisy beater car is burning oily smoke in your driveway. "Yo." He murmurs. He pushes past you and yells up the stairs to your daughter "Hurry up! My team is waiting for me on Xbox live. Our tournament starts in 10 minutes." Fantasy deflated. The rug is muddied with boot prints while it's being pulled out from under you. What exactly was the plan here?

There wasn't one. We seem to be in a kind of cultural crisis in this country. In an attempt to "lighten up" our parental attitudes about everything, we have cultivated an environment where our kids' highest goal is to "hang out." In general, there's nothing wrong with "hanging out." Letting your kids and their friends forage through your house for snacks, play video games, and watch movies builds social skills and teaches them how to get along with each other. BUT when it comes to dating, it is not good enough to say, "I'm going out with Jimmy." Oh, what are you guys going to do? "Oh, you know, just hang out." Oh, no you're not.

If your teen says, "I want to go driving with Sarah. Can I have the keys?" Oh? Where are you going? "Oh, you know, just around." No you're not. Does this sound healthy and rational? No, this sounds like a trip to Troublesville, and who's paying for the gas?

Dates have to be planned. Take Sarah to the diner for breakfast. Have a predetermined time for pick-up and drop off. Go for an hour to get ice cream. Invite her over for dinner. Here's a thought: your teen can help you cook the meal! You can gain all kinds of "cool parent" points from an evening like this. After a night of cooking with your teen, and then entertaining the date with a rousing game of Euchre, you could probably jump up a level to über Parent.

A well-spent dating hour should not only be planned, it needs to involve the opportunity for actually getting to know one another. You can't just plunk down in front of a movie and call it a date. Which brings us to the second crucial aspect of logging hours:

Dates must be intentional.
As a parent, you have earned the right to ask, "So what have we learned today, Dorothy?" We are "forcing" our oh-so-put-upon-teen to log hours for one intended reason: so that they can truly get to know this person with whom they are smitten. If your teen comes home after a date and you ask her, "So tell me about Brutus. What is he like?" And she says, "I don't know. He's got a great moustache." Not a lot of (healthy) learning took place.

> ➡ **You don't learn much just sitting in a car on the showroom floor.**

You need to teach your teen that dates are almost like fact-finding missions. (Stop for a minute to think about this: if you, as a parent, were somehow thrust into the dating world right now, what would you do on a first date? Believe me, you'd spend it asking your new beau all kinds of questions, up to and including what his relationship with his family is like and what he wants to do with the rest of his life.)

It seems so obvious, but the best way to get to know each other is to talk to each other. Have real conversations. Let's teach our kids how to ask open-ended questions so that they can engage in effective conversation. (This is a skill that will help them throughout their whole lives in every relationship. Maybe even a job interview.)

Some of you parents might remember "The Dating Game" from the ˋ60's. Three guys vied for the chance to date a girl hidden behind a wall. (Or three girls and one guy — equal opportunity pairings with host Jim Lange.) The girl had to choose her date based on questions she asked the hidden guys. "If you could design the perfect date, how would it start?" Bachelor number one: "Our perfect date would begin with the sky opening up, and butterscotch drops raining down from heaven. We'd sail off to an island picnic in a glass-bottomed boat."

The chooser had no idea what the dates looked like. She had to pick a date based only on his responses and not on what he looked like. ("Sorry, bachelor number one. I'm a diabetic and I can't swim. You should have done your research.") In this game, appearance was irrelevant to the decision.

Getting to know someone requires that you ask them questions that teach you something about that person. Good conversation uses open ended questions. An open-ended question is one that requires more than a "yes" or "no" answer. (Hold your sarcasm, wise guys. "Maybe" and "I don't know" don't count either.)

Model It...

Teaching your student to ask open-ended questions that require more than "yes" or "no" is a valuable

communication skill. Here are two ways to ask essentially the same question that yields very different results:

Question: "Do you like road trips?"

Answer: "Yes."

Well, that was effective. What have you learned? The person answering might think a road trip is driving 30 miles to find good salsa.

Try it this way (open-ended):

Question: "How would you describe a perfect road trip?"

Answer: "The perfect road trip is driving three days across the vast American plains to a little town in south Texas where they make the greatest salsa in the western hemisphere."

Now you're getting somewhere. With an open-ended question, the answer cannot be "yes" or "no." Help your student learn to ask questions that begin with "Who, What, When, Where, or How." ("Describe" or "Tell me" work well, too.) The idea is not to interrogate someone but to genuinely take an interest in who they are as a person. ("Brett, what was it like living in Uzbekistan growing up?") ("Kristen, why did you decide to write a paper on the possible extinction of the Piping Plover?")

➡ **Don't just be interesting... be interested.**

Asking open-ended questions is a great way for your student to find out more about someone and not just drool over their looks. It is a way to step into someone's world and see what makes them tick, to see beyond their physical beauty and decide how to pursue this relationship after that first thrilling glance.

Our culture has successfully trained our kids to communicate instantaneously with pictures and sounds. I've overheard entire conversations consisting of just a few words:

"Hey."

"Dude!!"

"Lame."

"Dude...?"

"Ha!"

This might be cool and concise but what have we learned? Is "Dude" mad? Does the "Hey" guy have a bad leg? They could have asked open-ended questions and gotten way more information:

"Hey, why are you chillin' by my car?"

"Dude, I'm so excited to see you! Where do you want to hang out?"

"The concession stand. I'm starving. My lunch was lame."

"Dude, got money?"

"Ha! Spent it all on Jen."

Well, why didn't you say so in the first place! I thought maybe "Dude" was mad at "Hey" and then laughed at him for no reason. Turns out, Jen only likes "Dude" for his looks and his wallet. She has never talked to him long enough to find out that his dad is an Ambassador of Switzerland where "Dude" spent the first seven years of his life. He speaks three languages (in complete sentences) and has a black belt in karate. Jen is more interested in his new credit card.

Model It...

To expand the point of the one-syllable and a pointless exchange, try this the next time your student asks "Do you know what time it is?" Simply answer, "Yes," and see how they respond. Not enough info, was it? Have a conversation about that. Next, pick a word in your own vocabulary that you tend to overuse. Ask your teen (maybe even your family) to count how many times in one day you use (or abuse) the word. The next day it can be your student's turn. (It might very well be the word "like." It's like the most overused word in, like, the entire country.)

The revealing of a personality usually takes much longer than this, of course. It takes hours of conversation to uncover one of two things:

1. This person has habits or character concerns that you might not be able to get past in a dating relationship… or:

2. This person continues to reveal to you a marvelous depth of character and you are falling more deeply in "like" by the syllable.

You might be thinking "Yea, right, ten hours of conversation is easy for girls but it would be torture for guys." Actually, I have found that given the opportunity, guys are just as willing to have good conversation. In fact, it fills the space when they can't think of anything else to do. Don't pry, but be interesting. Some people have a harder time opening up than others and if you just ask yes or no questions, you won't learn about their interests.

> **Every "pre-owned" car has a history.**
> **Every person has a story.**

Teach your student to be curious with tact. Keep it interesting. Would they rather drive 500 miles through the Mojave Desert or take the scenic route through the Rocky Mountains? Who has better salsa? Kids don't want to go on a monotonous drive for hours on end any more than they want to talk to an uninspiring person for hours. ("Hey Robby, I can't think of anything else to ask you and you bore me. Can we put on a romantic movie so I can feel like I'm in love?") There are all kinds of terrain on a road trip, and in dating too. Encourage your student to be unique and enjoy the journey.

Here is another great tip... keep first dates short. This gives your student time to step away from the emotion to regroup. ("Just to the store and back and we'll see how you do. And remember, look both ways.") Date in "regular" places under "regular" conditions. Every date is not the prom. Encourage your student to be real and not put on a façade. It's just a matter of time before their hair is dirty, the clothes are sloppy, and the attitude stinks. ("I let Jimmy kiss me at the dance because he was so cute in his tux. I had no idea that he wears the same T-shirt every weekend and that's not gel in his hair.") Every car from the showroom floor will at some point have hard miles, dirt, dents, repair, and maintenance issues just like the rest.

Talk with your teen about how they plan to log those first 10 hours to get to know their potential date. Are they going to play a video game for 9 hours or take a walk to the park? Help them mix it up and change the view. Time, and lots of it, will be their best ally in this dating drama. Your student should have every opportunity to step back and give themselves some time to come down from that initial visual high. That perfect specimen they collided with during those first staggering moments of attraction may disintegrate after even casual use. One pothole or mud puddle might just blur their illusion. It's easy to be sold on something we see for the first time if it has been highly polished and prepped for that one viewing. Unlike at the Prom, students don't present their best side every day and may not ever look like Prom Royalty again. Take off your tiara, get muddy, and see if he still likes you.

> ➲ **We don't live life on the Paris runway.**
> **We live on dirt roads and blacktop.**

A slower speed will increase your student's traction control. They start Driver's training plugging along at 30 miles per hour, not racing on the Autobahn. There is no reason for a Student Dater to plunge right into hugging turns during the first 10 hours they log. Once they are confident navigating the world of relationships, they will get better at defining what they want for the long haul, not just at the drive-thru. If they jump into the first car they see, they will be miserable with what they end up with. Conversation helps to reveal the personality traits of your date. This is how you find out whether you really have anything in common beyond mutual slobber.

Make logging intentional hours a reality. Your teen needs to spend quality and quantity time with his or her potential date. Engage in conversation and teach them to do the same. Invite the prospect over to meet the screw-loose parents. The key is to get their heads out of the clouds after that initial thrilling jolt. Let time and a little common sense keep them heading in the right direction. Sit on the porch and do a personality profile together. If they can take their eyes off the scenery and look ahead toward where they are going, they might actually get somewhere.

🏠 Drive It Home...

DIA-LOG with your student during the next 10 hours logged...

Getting to know you:

Play 20 questions.
One person thinks of something (a person, place, or thing) and the other person tries to guess it by

asking only "yes" or "no" questions. Talk about how boring or frustrating it can be to have a one-sided conversation. Ask them if they were ready to give up at any point. People want to know that you are interested in them but you shouldn't have to drag their personalities out of them.

Apply it to an actual date:

Your student is at a coffee shop with a date. He asks: "Do you like sports?" She says "Yes." He's on cloud nine because he thinks they have something in common, and he can go home and brag to mom. But here is the reality: your student is hooked on college sports and has season tickets to every basketball, football and hockey game at the local college. The girl meant, "Yes," she likes to play tennis, beach volleyball, and watch World Cup Soccer on TV. Does it sound like they have much in common so far?

Instead of asking meaningless, dead end questions, try using some of these questions during your first 10 hours logged. Help your student create his or her own list of questions based on the top five things he or she cannot live without. By starting conversations on topics that are interesting to your student, they will find out early on what kind of match this really is.

- What do you like best about school?
- What is your favorite thing to do in your spare time?
- What's your favorite movie of all time?
- If you could go anywhere on vacation, where would it be?
- How would you describe your family?
- What do you do to celebrate the holidays?

Volley. Ask a question that does not have a yes or no answer. The other person answers your question, then immediately has to ask you another question that is not "yes" or "no." See how long you can keep it up: 30 seconds, 1 minute, 3 minutes, 5 minutes...

Example:
Cindy: "James, how old were you when you moved here?"

James: "I was six. How long have you lived in this town, Cindy?"

Cindy: "Only three years. How many brothers and sisters do you have?" ...

Road Test...

Student:
Dates must be planned ahead of time. Here are some suggestions that you can utilize for your first date.

Invite a date over to play cards or a board game.

Sit across from each other and have a snack.

Watch a track meet or a soccer game.

Have a meal with your parents or theirs.

Go to a playground and go down the slide. Try the teeter totter. Avoid fat jokes.

Take a walk through your neighborhood.

Add five more to the list:
1. _____

2. _____

3. _____

4. _____

5. _____

Purchase or design a Log Sheet or journal. (See _Chapter 3—"Logging Hours."_) Reference it often.

Read Your Manual!

A boy was walking along a country road when he came across a talking girl frog. "Pick me up and kiss me and I'll turn into the most beautiful girl you have ever seen. All your friends will be envious and jealous because you will have me as your gorgeous girlfriend."

The boy looked at the frog for a short time, reached over, picked it up carefully, and placed it in his shirt pocket.

Then the girl frog said, "What, are you nuts? Didn't you hear what I said? I said kiss me and I will be your very own beautiful girlfriend."

The boy opened his pocket, looked at the frog and said, "Nah, I'd rather have a talking frog."

10 Sign, Sign, Everywhere a Sign

When I lived in Denver, Colorado, I owned a cute little red Mazda truck. I lived in a nice suburban neighborhood at the top of a steep suburban hill. It was winter, and on this particular night there was a blizzard warning, which meant "don't go out." This is Colorado. We mean it. But it was also Achy-Breaky night at the Charlie Horse Saloon, and nothing was going to keep me from line dancing. The minute the TV said the weather advisory was cancelled, I put on my denim skirt and ruby red snake skin boots and headed out my suburban door.

There were signs everywhere that this was a bad idea but I was too blind to see them. I should have stopped when I had to unbury the car with a shovel. I should have stopped when I could only clear a Texas-belt-buckle-sized circle of ice off the windshield. I should have stopped when my wheels spun backing out of the driveway. But no, I had a new cowgirl hat and I was going out.

Even as I headed down that hill, I knew there would be trouble later making it home, but still I kept going. And going. And going. There was a STOP sign at the end of that steep road, but stopping was not going to happen. I stood on my brakes with both boots and held my breath as my little truck slid toward the busy intersection. It didn't quite make it. I slid right up over the curb and hit the STOP sign dead on, bending the pole to almost parallel with the ground. The wheels were spinning freely above the snow, the front-end was suspended in midair over the STOP sign. The snow fell, the radiator hissed. Call it luck, call it creative. That STOP sign did the job.

The State of Michigan Driver's Handbook lists and describes some of the most common traffic signs that a driver will encounter on the road. These signs are not just posted so that "the big man" can control "the little people." They are not just an easy way for the government to keep us in line, to stifle our youthful exuberance. No, traffic signs are not just the law, they are a brilliant idea. They keep us safe, they keep us whole, they keep us from flying into the lap of an oncoming cattle hauler. Sometimes, if we pay attention to them, they'll even keep us from running smack dab into, say, a STOP sign.

The government posts these signs, and it's the driver's job to watch for them, interpret them and obey them. Some road signs are gentle reminders — Curve Ahead. Some require a quicker, more critical adjustment — Road Closed — Bridge Out.

Reading road signs during dating is a little trickier because the signs aren't posted where you would like them to be. And they are often obscured by the fog of emotional involvement. Your student might not recognize what appear to be clear signs to the rest of us out here in the "unimpaired zone." If a guy sees his girlfriend leaning against her locker, twirling her hair, and flirting with another guy from her math class, *we* all see an "I'm thinking about cheating" sign, while your love-blind student sees what pretty hair she has. Every individual will respond differently to these dating symbols depending on their maturity and personality. If a girl catches her underage boyfriend drinking alcohol, she may or may not recognize the bright, flashing warning sign that says "Unemployed party-boy ahead. Detour recommended."

As your student begins to date, you must frequently check in on them to see what they're learning on this new relationship road. Once they have logged 10 hours with one person, you need to dig a little deeper into the warnings that will inevitably appear when two people have begun to create a real relationship. Let's take a look at some common road signs and see how we can apply those to our student's dating education. We will look at four different categories of signs: regulatory, warning, guide, and signals. This verbiage is taken directly from the *State of Michigan Driver's Ed Study Guide.* Anything you see in *bold italics*, I didn't make up.

Our state manual says that *"REGULATORY SIGNS"* are usually red and white or black and white. They are used to *"control moving traffic"* but they are, more importantly, *"a way to communicate."* So what do they "communicate" to our students? Let's take a look.

YIELD — *"Driver must slow down and prepare to stop if necessary. Give way to traffic and pedestrians."*

When merging into traffic, you slow down, let others pass, then merge when there is an opening. Does this remind you of the halls at school? A student might only have four minutes to get from one class to the next. Pay attention to your date as he or she weaves in and around the crowd to get to geometry. Does he shove his way through and slam into people that get in his path? Can you pick out a gentleman in the chaos? He's the one holding the door. Is your date lady-like and polite or is she a princess with a "me first" royal strut?

Yielding when you drive means recognizing that you are not the only car on the road. It's common courtesy. (Maybe not so common anymore.) In dating, it might mean that your student can't see his sweetie every night of the week. Your student has homework, chores, sports, and a job that require his time. Your teen undoubtedly has a set of friends that he should not have to ditch just because he has a new girl. Is she taking it slow and letting other "pedestrians" have some time with your student? Little Miss Manners needs learn to "share the road" and model good etiquette along the way.

Model It...

YIELD. At dinner, gently push ahead of your child and sit in their "regular" seat. Chew with your mouth open.

Reach across the dinner table for the potatoes. Elbow them occasionally. See if your student notices (duh!) and then have a conversation about common courtesy, manners, and personal space. What kind of behaviors do we demonstrate that broadcast how we tend to treat others? Discuss what signs a teen can look for in their dates that indicate that they have the capacity to "yield" to those around them.

STOP—"You must come to a complete stop behind a certain line."

After your student has logged some quality hours with another student, chances are they will run into a STOP sign or two. (Hopefully not a truck-bending real one.) What has your student asked someone else to stop doing? Chewing with their mouth open? ("I only want to see the broccoli going in, my friend.") What has someone else asked your student to stop doing? ("Stop calling after hours.") ("Please don't ignore me when your friends are around.") In dating, this might be called the "Stop That" sign.

> **Would it take a red octagon painted on your student's forehead before their date got the message?**

Model It...

STOP. Sing in a public place or at home - loud and off key. Act out your student's pet peeve (speak in that horrible British accent when you're with her friends). Do it until your student asks (or begs!) you to stop. Dialogue about the things in a relationship that can be irritating or make your student uncomfortable. What needs to stop? ("Still chewing on your hair? Has Doug been trying to tell you that it makes him think of cat hairballs?") Brainstorm with them on how to tactfully let the other student know what the problem is. You don't just shout, "Brian! Would you quit texting me?!" There is a much gentler way to suggest to someone that you need a break from something. Never underestimate the power of an initial compliment to soften some criticism. "Brian, you know I love texting you, but after 10:00 I really need my beauty rest. You don't want me to sleep through Calculus class, do you? Can we agree to end our convos by 10:00? Besides, that will keep my mother off my back, too." Shift appropriate blame to the parents. We'll let you.

DO NOT ENTER and WRONG WAY

Have you ever been traveling down a narrow one-way street and there's someone coming the other way, right toward you? What are they doing there? How could they have missed the sign? Or did they see the sign but choose to ignore it, thinking only that they wanted to be in *this* alley at *this* time and nothing was going to get in their way? We teach our kids to just say "No," but they don't always master the technique or use a loud or convincing enough voice. Is your student's date ignoring a sign that is clearly marked "DO NOT ENTER"? ("How many times do I have to tell him to stop coming to my dance class?") Maybe a student continues to press your child for information on a private matter. DO NOT ENTER.

Model It...

DO NOT ENTER. Sit down with your student and his friends on the couch while they are playing video games. Answer their cell phone before they can get to it and watch the disturbing looks you will get. Talk about privacy and the space your student needs. What things should they be able to focus on without distractions? What aspects of their lives should they expect to perform

without the boyfriend or girlfriend always showing up? Job, schoolwork, lessons, church, family time...

The "WRONG WAY" is an equally important regulatory sign. ("I've told you before that I am not ready for that kind of relationship!") What if your student keeps getting notes from their crush during class and that gets them in trouble? That's the WRONG WAY. Maybe the date doesn't want to hold your student's hand. We must teach our children to both give clear signs and to read the signs of others clearly.

Model It...

WRONG WAY. Call your own child on their cell at 3:00am and see if you get a rise out of them. Does their new "friend" call them at that hour? Then why can't you? Talk about how easy it is to identify when someone has rubbed you the wrong way. Discuss what behaviors are off-limits. Talk about not compromising just to avoid a conflict.

> **If the signs are not perfectly clear, ask directions or don't go down that road.**

DO NOT PASS and PASS WITH CARE

This is an entire chapter all by itself; in fact, it is discussed in depth in *Chapter 11: "Boundary Lines."* For now, we will just skim the surface of the explanation of these posted signs.

What happens when you try to pass when you're not supposed to? In a word, BOOM! If you can't see what's coming around the bend, I hope you enjoy the smell of plaster and the feel of full-body traction. "DO NOT PASS" signs are mounted to warn you: "Hey, don't even think about it. If you pass and crash into that Chevy pick-up that's barreling over the hill, you can't say we didn't warn you. This is going to hurt."

Model It...

> *DO NOT PASS.* Be a "close-talker." Stand six inches closer to your student than you normally do. How does that make them feel? It is critical to establish physical boundaries at the very beginning of a relationship. Stand firm on your expectations before you are in over your head. Create an obvious "DO NOT PASS" sign from day one.

A "PASS WITH CARE" sign might be mounted on the bride's door, but it is an unacceptable marker to display during dating. Make it clear to your vulnerable teen: stay in your own lane and "do not make a pass" until you are married. "PASSING" is dangerous business.

> **"*DO NOT PASS*" is a crystal clear "NO."**
> **It does not mean:**
> **"Well, ok, if you really feel like it."**

Driver's Ed teachers don't even let students *attempt* to PASS WITH CARE while they are in training. Why? A high-level of danger coupled with an abundance of naïveté = crash + ruin. When you are a beginning dater, the same formula should be put into effect. Play it safe. ("I never feel safe around Chip because he always tries to make a pass at me.") DO NOT PASS. Point out to your student that even on the road, when the state determines that it's a safe stretch of road on which to pass, it is still marked PASS WITH CARE. Why? Because you better take care to look ahead at what's coming the other way and never take your eyes off the goal of arriving safely. PASS WITH CARE is not a big green light. It does not mean "floor it with disregard."

Model It...

PASS WITH CARE. Talk about abstinence from a driver's point of view. While driving with your teen, point out the places in the road where it is dangerous to pass. Ask your student what is at risk if they pass without knowing what is ahead. Ask them to study the front end of a Mack truck, and then ask them if they'd like the impression of that grill emblazoned on their foreheads. Be clear that a marriage license is the best indicator that you can *"PASS WITH CARE."*

SPEED LIMIT

When you drive, you constantly monitor your speed. Speed limits can change frequently within short distances. Going less than the speed limit can be annoying and incite others to road rage. ("I have been waiting two years for Josh to ask me out. I feel like we are in neutral going nowhere. Maybe I'll just go around him.") Speeding is particularly dangerous for both young drivers and inexperienced daters. Their control system is not yet prepared for rushing down the dating highway. ("Kristine moves way too fast. I want to steer clear of that reputation.")

> **Who will take control of the speed and keep their foot on the brake?**

In what areas is your student moving too fast or too slowly? Do they call 47 times a day or once a month? Does your student beat their date to their locker between every class? Did they try to plant an unwanted kiss? In the same way that speed limits vary around town, set limits for various environments so that your student knows what is and is not a safe rate of speed. ("I can go to the Dairy Queen but Dad said "no" to the Mosh Pit.")

Model It...

SPEED LIMIT. Drive under the speed limit and watch as the tension in the car rises. Point out the reactions from other drivers. Count how many people offer you unwanted gestures. If you were to whip quickly around a blind curve, would your student speak up about how uncomfortable that is? Talk about the "safe speed" in a relationship. Would the Prom be a good first date? (Here's a subtle hint: NO! NO! Just say no! That's like driving the Detroit Grand Prix for your first road test.)

WARNING SIGNS — "These signs are used to alert the driver of any unusual activity or situations that would not otherwise be present."

ROAD WORK AHEAD — "Construction is an area that you need to pay close attention to."

Any time there is Road Work, this generally means there is some "destruction" before the "construction." It usually occurs in phases over a period of time. Example: widening a freeway starts with digging up the old road, leaving gaping holes perfect for to falling into and breaking an axle. Some students undergo periods of construction and reconstruction, especially during times of upheaval in a student's life. ("Kim's grades have really dropped and she is pretty discouraged.") ("Scott's parents just got a divorce. He's having a hard time with it.") Advise your student to approach these Road Work areas gently and with caution. Tread lightly and be ready to idle for periods of time. Remember, fines are doubled in work zones. If you injure someone while they are trying to repair their lives, that's like kicking them in a fresh wound. Bad move.

Model It...

ROAD WORK AHEAD. When you see road construction, talk about the all the changes that affect the normal routine. Be patient, slow down, back off, go around, stay away, be more alert, detour temporarily. It is critical in a relationship to recognize the magnitude of the change that might occur in a person's life when people are under construction. Talk about events that might cause destruction (divorce, school work, death, illness). Discuss how long and how involved the resulting re-construction might take.

CURVE AHEAD — "This sign indicates that the road ahead is going to take a turn that is going to limit your visibility and head you in a different direction than the way you have gotten used to. In addition, it will mean you have to slow down."

Is there an upcoming event in your student's life that may throw their date a curve? A big exam? A competition? A date with someone else? ("Heather is really stressing over her Trig final.") ("Justin is so nervous about the audition for the school play that all he does is recite Shakespeare morning till night.") Part of Driver's Ed is learning how to handle curves. Step one: slow down as you approach the curve. Staying alert is critical to navigating the new landscape. Your student will face curves on the roads of their relationships many times. Learning to stay calm and stay focused even though the visibility is limited requires practice. Pay attention.

Model It...

CURVE AHEAD. This is different from road work. Road work comes and goes. Curves are constant and have far fewer and less obvious warning signs. In a curve, visibility will be limited until the straightaway. Discuss the reality that curves occur on every road, in any relationship. Discuss how to proceed with caution.

GUIDE SIGNS — "These signs are blue and show what is available ahead indicating some distance, destination and direction."

REST AREA
Does your student need to take a break from the relationship? Are they checking all their gauges? Most rest areas have maps and, well, a place to rest. Have your student stop and check their course and desired destination. Are both the student and the date headed in the same direction? Are they on track? Do they need to refuel? ("Michael is suffocating me. I need some time to breathe and think about whether this is what I want.") ("Paige is so busy with Marching Band and soccer. We just need to chill for a month or so.")

Model It...

REST AREA. Pull into a rest area and point out the differences between rest areas and a Mike's Super Truck Stop. (The rest area is quieter, it offers less distraction.) You don't stop at a rest area to eat, shop, or look at a big ball of twine. You are there to take a break. Talk about how healthy it is to just stop and rest occasionally. Breathe in some fresh air.

SIGNALS — "Generally used when a sign is not enough. They are typically used in combination with pavement markings indicating a line you do not cross."

GREEN LIGHT
Is that really a green light your student's date is sending? Green is an invitation to proceed, in both directions.

Model It...

When you are at an intersection, does the light usually turn green in just one direction? No. Traffic will move forward in both directions. Communication and commitment are far more successful when both parties proceed on the same green light.

YELLOW LIGHT

Did the signal just change? Did one party just hesitate a little bit? At a yellow light, you must decide whether to go forward or stop. When is a yellow just a yellow, and when is it slightly orange?

Model It...

At a yellow light, you can either brake or floor it. Discuss which is safer. Be alert and recognize when things might unexpectedly be put on hold for a time or not happen as quickly as expected. Maybe the person they wish to date has already said yes to someone else for Prom. No problem. Wait it out. Their turn will come. Idle in anticipation.

RED LIGHT—Full stop!!!!!!!

Is your student creeping past the line anticipating a green light? Does their nose stick out beyond the safety zone just waiting to get flattened?

Model It...

Come to a full and complete **STOP** at a red light. Not rolling, not a tap on the brakes, but **DO NOT MAKE A MOVE**. Talk about respecting someone's flashing red light and not going one inch over the mark.

Constantly reading signs is a crucial part of driving safety. It is of no less importance when it comes to dating. Dating signs are not written in large block reflective print, but if we teach our teens some of the obvious things to look for, they are less likely to run off the road onto someone's lawn. Even if you've been driving for 10 years, you still read the signs. Ever been driving on an unfamiliar freeway when the temperature suddenly drops and the rain turns to sleet? Those signs that say "Bridge freezes before road surface" suddenly become crucial to staying alive. Relationships change just like road conditions change. Whether you've been dating for 10 days or 10 years, you must still watch for signs so you can arrive safely.

 Drive It Home...

DIA-LOG with your student during the next 10 hours logged...

Road Trip...

Student in the driver's seat – Parents observe and discuss your student's answers to the following questions regarding signs:

Yield
- What examples can you give of your date's manners?
- Are they polite? Do they consistently say "Please" and "Thank you"?
- Does he open the car door for you? Does she walk 10 paces ahead?
- How do you feel he/she respects your time with your friends, homework, and personal time?

- Describe how your date adds to your social life or puts up roadblocks.

Stop

- Are there any particular behaviors that aggravate or annoy you?
- How often do you need to say "Stop that"?
- What pet peeves do they have that bother you?
- Give an example of how your date recognizes when something bothers you.

Do Not Enter

- In what ways does your date respect your privacy and commitments?
- Give an example of how your date understands the need to be invited (or not) to your personal events.

Wrong Way

- List three examples of how your date is pursuing you the right way.
- Define the problem areas that are taking you off course and just don't feel right.

Do Not Pass

- How do you feel about your date flirting with you?
- Explain how the flirting could easily cross the line into a "pass."

Pass With Care

- What are your date's morals when it comes to physical touch and sex?
- Have you had a conversation that your date understands and respects?

Speed Limit
- Which one of you seems to be going faster in this relationship?
- Give examples of occurrences when you and your date traveled at different speeds. Did that make you uncomfortable?

Road Work Ahead
- Describe what large, emotional projects might be going on in their lives that could affect the relationship.
- What events may have happened in the student's past from which he or she might still be rebuilding?

Curve Ahead
- List anything you can think of that might be on their mind right now that could throw you a curve: perhaps an upcoming event that could change the direction of your relationship.
- What is the best course of action in response to this information?

Rest Area
- How would you describe the stress level when you are dating?
- How would it feel to take a short break from dating?

Green Light
- What clues has your date given you that you are compatible?

Yellow Light
- Describe how you read your date's moods and responses to you.

Red Light
- How would you recognize when the relationship needs to come to a full stop?
- How would you feel if that happened?

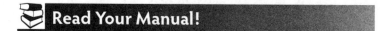 **Read Your Manual!**

A guy returns to his parked BMW to find the headlights broken and considerable damage to the front end. There's no sign of the car that hit him but he's relieved to see that there's a note stuck under the windshield wiper.

"Sorry. I just backed into your Beemer. The witnesses who saw the accident are smiling at me right now because they think I'm leaving my name, address and other particulars. But I'm not. See ya!"

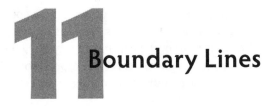

11 Boundary Lines

I was heading east on a four-lane highway in Vista, California. The speed limit was 65, but traffic started to jam up and slow to a crawl for no visible reason. The right lane appeared to move a little faster than the left, so I pulled into it. Finally I neared the cause of the traffic jam and had to laugh out loud.

In the left lane was a shiny new red sports car going about 45 miles an hour. Driving it was a sweet but ancient Asian man with a death grip on the steering wheel. He could barely see over the dash board at all the chaos he was causing. Folks were laying on their horns and flashing him their special gestures as they flew by him, but he was unbothered. Then I figured out why. His license plate said it all. It was a vanity plate — given to him probably by his grandchildren when they discovered that he bought himself a toy he could not control. It said: **"NO RUN N2"**! This was their way of keeping him safe. Now *that's* funny.

Please don't hit Gramps, even though he crossed way over the line driving a car he had no business owning, in the fast lane on a freeway struggling to keep up. His inexperience and lack of ability clearly did not match the image of the Indy driver he had for himself.

Being a good driver is as much about learning where *to* go as where *not* to go. When you first learn to drive, you spend a great deal of energy just trying to stay between the lines (reminiscent of coloring in kindergarten). There's a white line on your right side that says, "don't go in this ditch." There's a yellow line on your left side that says, "don't cross me." White lines in parking lots say "park in between these." Blue lines in the parking lot say, "Are you absolutely *sure* that you qualify to park in this handicapped zone?" Lines painted in the road define boundaries telling us where *to* keep our vehicle and where *not* to.

> ### Don't prepare the path for the child, prepare the child for the path.

As you log more driving hours, you realize that the lines in the middle of the road are either solid or dotted, which means sometimes it is okay to pass, and sometimes it isn't. And even when the lines are solid double yellow meaning, "Do not pass, I am *so* not kidding," you still get to choose. The road commission did not erect a concrete wall down the center of that road. It's just a painted line. You have to *choose* not to cross. Which means you could, if you have a death wish, make the choice to cross over the yellow lines, even when you shouldn't.

And this makes sense. What if you're driving down a darkened two-lane road at night that has a well-marked stretch of the double-yellow "DO NOT PASS" lines, and you need to turn left into your Uncle Ken's country cabin in the woods? Well, you'd put on your signal, peer as far down the road as possible, watch for crazy attack deer, and turn left after the traffic cleared. A double yellow line is a suggestion, not a barrier. We have free will. We get to choose.

What if, however, you're driving down that same dark stretch of road, and your buddy is head-banging next to you blaring the latest alternative CD. You're coming up a steep hill and find yourself quickly approaching the unmistakable triangular reflection of a "slow-moving vehicle" sign on the back of a John Deere™ tractor. Immediately, your wiser-than-words friend challenges you. "You can take this cornhusker. Go for it!" You can't see over the hill, and your manhood has been tested. What do you do? It's a double yellow line. It won't STOP you from veering over into oncoming traffic. It's not a barrier, just a suggestion.

But it's a good one. Because coming up the other way is a logging truck driven by a guy whose CB handle is Earl the Pearl, who's aching to get home and put his feet up in front of the football game. So, what do you think? Should you cross that line anyway because your buddy is daring you to or should you stay on your side because clearly the boundary is marked as "stay in your lane— even if it's frustrating and your buddy thinks you're a dweeb"? Believe it or not, you will get to the top of the hill very shortly, and you will get to pass as soon as traffic has cleared. What would you take in this trade: a few minutes of frustration or six months of reconstructive facial surgery?

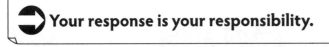

Your response is your responsibility.

There are four categories of boundaries that define the limits of who we are and what we "allow" from our dates, our partners, or our friends: physical, emotional, financial, and spiritual/moral. In dating, setting these boundaries early is crucial. Knowing where the lines are drawn right from the start gives your student the opportunity to strengthen their own personal boundaries as they log hours with potential dates, *before* they become a broken casualty. An experienced driver can "stay within the lines" even when the paint is faded or missing altogether. (Ever driven when the road is covered with snow and you can't even see the center? Or on a dirt road where there *is* no center line?) You can still make intelligent decisions about how far to drift to the left, or whether or not to pass on a hill, even when the roads aren't marked. In this chapter we will explore how to teach your teen which boundary lines are solid meaning "do not cross" and which ones are dotted, implying "occasionally cross with caution."

Let's start with the physical boundaries.

Ten and two. If you have taken Driver's Ed, you know exactly what this means. Keep your hands positioned at ten o'clock and two o'clock on the steering wheel at all times while driving. There are good reasons for this rule:

1. You have the greatest control over the car this way. You can control it left, you can control it right. You can control it a little ("Sweetie, you see that mailbox? You're just a hair over the shoulder line.") You can control it a lot. ("Sweetie, that dump truck is bigger than you are. Please steer right... Now!")

2. If both hands are on the wheel, they can't be busy doing something which could mean trouble. How many accidents have been caused by Jeremy fishing under the seat for his iPod™? Keep your hands on the wheel, in control where they belong, eyes up on the road.

🚶 Model it...

How would your teen react if they watched you open their purse, backpack, or dresser drawer and took something out that didn't belong to you? My teens would yell, "What are you doing! Stay out of there!" Talk to your student about respecting other people's boundaries. Discuss what you can and cannot touch. An example of a **solid line** might be that anyone else's bedroom other than your own (alone) is strictly off limits at all times. A **dotted line** might be specific instructions not to go in someone else's refrigerator unless you are given permission to do so.

We have been taught not to touch other people's things since we were kids. Did any one else have a little sister who constantly wanted to wear her sweaters and borrow her prized collection of "Laugh-In" stickers? As we get older, our toys get bigger, and our "stuff" gets more expensive. Discussing the rules about "touching my stuff" can become quite impassioned.

➔ Don't touch the merchandise!

Let me illustrate this point. Every year in the heat of August, a million people line the streets of Royal Oak, Michigan, to watch the "Woodward Dream Cruise." From muscle cars to classic cars, from Model T's to dragsters, the show is a 16-mile, two-day parade of the hottest, most well preserved automobiles in the world. Visitors camp out for days in advance to get a front row lawn chair on the curb. (Nostrils meet exhaust.) Car owners come to town a week before parade day and park their "babies" in show lots for the public to drool over. Or should I say, drool *nearby*. Because you can look all you want at these gorgeous vehicles, but touching is off limits. The owners have spent countless hours restoring and perfecting their investment, and *you may not touch*.

So how much more vigilant should teens be with their most prized possessions—themselves? At the Woodward Dream Cruise the obvious message is: *Don't Paw the Body*. Our teen's billboard should state: *Don't Paw the Body*. Does your student think it's ok to leave fingerprints on the merchandise? Your student should know what it means to respect other people's physical property and their boundaries. Does your student have a clear idea where the lines are drawn? This is not the place for gray areas or faded lines. In fact, why not use "tan lines" as a kind of guide for what is ok to touch, and what is not? If it might get tan, you can touch it. If it never sees the sun, Do Not Paw. (And I mean tan lines from a one-piece bathing suit from the 1940's for girls, not a thong.)

➔ Even if you are Italian, you shouldn't have "Roman hands."

So, where should your student's hands be when they are on a date? Not on the date, you hope! Sometimes keeping hands out of trouble means occupying them with some other distraction. You can keep your hands in your pockets, carry a worry stone, or fidget with your school ring. Temptation begins with just a thought, and when it is provoked by inappropriate touching, it can spiral out of control and boundaries may be crossed with unpleasant results. Keeping your hands busy can keep your temptations in check.

Model it...

Pinch your teen's nose and wait for the reaction. Play with their hair. Fix their collar. Talk about recognizing and respecting physical boundaries. Draw the lines for them.

Solid Line: Hands should never go where a reasonable bathing suit would cover. In other words, seriously limit "torso touching." Chaperone a high school dance. Yikes. Witnessing that level of clothed grinding and fondling will rev up your engine and inspire you to have a poignant conversation with your own teen. (And these are the kids being watched.)

Dotted Line: Hugging is acceptable when it is appropriate. Define "reasonable and appropriate" with your student. (A congratulatory squeeze or a goodbye hug—these can be good things if the hands remain "area appropriate.") Does tickling qualify? What about holding hands? Putting your arm around your date at the theatre? Discuss how drivers are more likely to have an accident if their hands are not on the wheel but are somewhere else fiddling with some other distraction.

Even as experienced drivers, do we always have both hands on the wheel? ("Have you seen Aunt Grace drive with her elbow and change stations with her toe?") And it's not just our hands that relax when we drive. I've seen people speeding down the freeway, lounging in their driver's seat like it's a La-Z-Boy™

recliner, one finger on the wheel at 6:00, the other hand wrapped around a Mountain Dew in their lap. Do they realize that they are pulverizing insects on their windshield at 75 miles an hour or is this just a virtual video screen to them? What about the folks who drive with one foot propped out the car window or hand surfing the rushing wind? It makes me want to sing the "Hokey Pokey" until all body parts are inside the vehicle.

High speed reclining is dangerous. You need hands, eyes, and feet to pay attention at all times. You need your eyes on all the mirrors and your feet poised above the pedals. Just ask Eddie Haskell. ("Gee willikers, Mrs. Cleaver; I can't imagine how I lost my penny loafer out the car window down on Lover's Lane.") My point here is that if the feet are off the ground, what's supporting the rest of the body? Are you grateful (like me) that they no longer sell cars with bench seats in front?

➲ Get off your seat and on your feet!

Apply this to dating. Once your feet are off the floor and you're lounging on the couch with your date, you're only one hip-shift away from lying prone. And prone is NOT a position you should pursue with your date. Who is in control if you're lying together on the couch? Where are your hands? Where are your eyes? What is your temptation level? Teach your teen that keeping it upright means keeping it all right. In fact, it is not a bad idea to suggest that teens just keep it moving. Get up, go for a walk, go for a run, climb rocks, even dance (fox trot, not grind.) Spend some of that teen dating energy working up a healthy sweat. My garage always needs sweeping.

👪 Model It...

Have your student sit on the coach with their feet on the ground. Ask them to lie down without raising their

feet off the floor. Would they feel safe driving in that position? Could they still reach the brakes? Keeping both feet flat on the floor at all times will keep you in control and allow you to stop when you need to, in both driving and dating. Define the boundaries for idle lounging time so that "hanging out" doesn't turn into "parking."

Solid Line: You cannot watch movies together in the dark.

Dotted Line: You can lie down to watch TV only if you are on separate couches. (And the parent reserves the right to enter the room at random and say "Ooh, this is the best scene ever. Can I watch for a minute with you guys?") Discuss whether daters can watch a movie together in the basement alone or the family room. Lights on or dimmed? Door closed or door always open? Rated PG or R?

Telling drivers when it's not safe to pass is such a critical instruction that the road commission posts the directive in more than one way. Not only are there DO NOT PASS signs posted on your right every few 100 meters, but there is also a solid line painted right down the middle of the road - a continual visual aid for drivers that indicates, "Hey, this bit of road is dangerous for passing, we really mean it." Solid line? The law says don't cross - not negotiable. Your student should have some solid lines written into their dating directive that keeps them from "passing" and putting themselves or others in physical danger.

Imagine a two lane paved country road. A double set of lines are painted down the center telling each direction of traffic whether they can pass or not. Sometimes they are both solid, sometimes only one is solid and one is dotted. Maybe oncoming traffic can pass but you can't. In dating, it is not uncommon that the other student's "passing zone" has different boundary lines than your student's. Discuss with your teen how another person's agenda or personal guidelines might not match their

Chapter 11: Boundary Lines

own interpretation of when it's okay to make a "pass" and what to do in that situation. Practicing a "knee-jerk" reaction (pun intended) to crossing physical boundaries might look like this: "Jeff, if you truly care about me, you will protect my physical integrity and respect my boundaries. I will do the same with you." Then... define the lines.

Lines are much easier to float across when nobody is looking. Say it's midnight, you're cruising home from a barbecue, it's just you, the ever-abiding deer, your crazy friend Jake in the passenger's seat, and miles of deserted roads. How tempting is it to edge those front wheels over that white line and yell, "Take that, Yank. I'm driving like a Londoner!" What a kick! We are far less tempted to take that same chance in rush hour traffic. Too crowded to take the risk. Let's relate that concept to dating and draw some healthy boundaries keeping the idea that "crowds are watching me" in mind.

Model It...

During a car ride with your teen in heavy traffic, talk about how risky it would be to cross the lines. (Do not demonstrate this. You're older and wiser, remember?) Discuss how much more tempting and "safer" it would be to fade across the line if you were the only one on the road. Crowds help keep you in your own lane.

Solid Line: The first three dates must be in a group of three or more in a well-lit public place. It takes two to Tango... not three or four... and that's one dance you don't want them doing. Suggest members of their Pit Crew that might go along.

Dotted Line: Once you feel confident about the integrity of your student's date, "let the clutch out" and allow them to go solo. Set a boundary that they always need to "date" in a public area and not alone on a couch. Tell them how you feel about them being home alone together... even for 1 minute. Help your student choose "group daters" in whom you have confidence, other students who understand and support this concept. Note: group dating is not foolproof, especially if the group is composed of less than admirable people. Friends are not chaperones.

> **The road commission doesn't paint solid lines around your personal life telling you not to cross. That's your job.**

On the street, a dotted line means it's safe to cross. Oncoming traffic can see you, you can see them. If the coast is clear, the risk is relatively low and passing is within the law. The lines on the road are black and white... not gray. When it comes to dating, those same lines need to be just as clearly marked.

And what are we really referring to when we say "passing"? You need to clearly define "sex" with your student. Does kissing count? Touching private parts over clothes? Getting naked but not going "all the way"? Just what exactly is over the line? Which of the following dotted-line words should dictate when it is okay to cross the line and have sex:

F-R-I-E-N-D-S

D-A-T-I-N-G

M-A-R-R-I-A-G-E

Let's face it; it's all about safety. The #1 requirement before you hand over the keys to your car is that you are *certain* your student is capable of protecting their own "physical integrity" and that of the other people they journey with through life. Shouldn't that be the #1 goal in dating? ("Hi, I'm Carlos and what I want more than anything is to 'protect your sexual reputation' whenever we are together.") That's what I'm talking about.

Defining a physical relationship is hard enough. (Even some of our most popular presidents have had trouble defining "sex.") It can be even tougher to define emotional boundaries in a relationship because feelings are so intangible.

We hope our children have healthy, loving relationships full of mutual support, friendship, laughter and even a sanctioned kiss or two. Teens have been watching and learning about relationships from their parents, friends, relatives but it doesn't stop there. Technology has more power to educate our students than all the teachers on the globe. And although we try diligently to instill self-confidence and strong family values in our kids, these are vulnerable and difficult years. Their sense of self-worth might be warped from... anything: movies, friends, hormones, misguided presidents. Kids are vulnerable and they might not always recognize when a relationship is unhealthy. That's why specific, measurable, definable boundaries lay the best foundation.

Any kind of manipulation, control, or abuse whether it's physical, verbal or emotional is not only dysfunctional, it must be downright forbidden. Watch your teens carefully for signs of relationship stress (hidden crying, fear, bruises). What might look like adoration to a naive teenager, ("He always wants to know where I am because he loves me,") can become in actuality an abusive situation. ("Man, he won't even let me go to cheerleading practice without texting me every five minutes.")

Let's offer our kids a model for dealing with unhealthy relationships.

Model It...

Use the TV remote to increase the volume from very soft to very loud and ask your teen to tell you when the noise level becomes offensive. Discuss how yelling, shouting, debating, and arguing look and feel.

Solid Line: Your teen will not under any circumstance be allowed to continue to date someone who is abusive or demeaning in any way. The parent has the final word on this, not the teen. Explain how you might recognize abuse. Every relationship will have its emotional challenges, but do not keep crossing the <u>dotted line</u> to save a reoccurring nightmare. ("This is the 5th date in a row Kara has come home crying.") ("Scott is obsessed with seeing his girlfriend every day, and now he's flunking Algebra.") Yes, sometimes a person may have a really bad day and kick the door. And we will forgive them.

Dotted Line: They do it twice, that dotted line solidifies. If they kick your teen, once, just once, that line is not only solid, it becomes a police line up. Abuse is no joke and can not be tolerated.

Because emotional boundaries are harder to define and even harder to discuss with an emotional teen (whose mood can alternate between door slamming and silent pouting) consider giving them a gift of counseling sessions or life-coaching for their birthday instead of a new iPod™. Give them tools they can use for the rest of their lives. (And that don't require an extended warranty.) Let a professional help your teen draw the lines emotionally. Remind them that this is not an insult. This does not mean that you don't trust them. It is instruction by a professional; it is a lesson just like piano or swimming. It makes you stronger and smarter and well-equipped to master one of toughest skills on earth: human relationships.

> ⏩ **Are your student's boundaries drawn in permanent paint or sidewalk chalk?**

OK. Let's shift gears. We talked about where dating money comes from in *Chapter 6: "Qualifying for Dater's Ed."* Now let's look at the boundaries surrounding cash (or heaven forbid, credit!). No matter where the money comes from (Bank of Dad or a McDonald's paycheck) there should be limits (boundaries) on spending for dates. There was a boy in my daughter's 2nd grade class who came to our house with his dad to give her a real diamond necklace. These kids were eight. She didn't even know his last name, and this kid was practically planning their engagement party.

Granted, different people live in different social strata (Buffy and Tiff might have more disposable income than, say, my entire bowling league.) But every teen should have some kind of suggested budget. They cannot spend their college fund on the soccer captain. Just like owning a car, dating can deplete your budget, especially if it's frivolous. ("Angelina saw how the other girls flocked to her man Collin because he was so 'hot,' so she bought a new wardrobe to keep him interested in her.")

No car and no relationship is maintenance free. It will wind up costing you money. Just keep the costs reasonable and sane. ("Mark competes constantly with the vultures hovering over his girl. He works two jobs to buy the pricey dinners and movies she 'needs' to feel pampered.") How much is too much? How much would you keep investing in a GM clunker with 300,000 miles on it? At some point, enough is enough, whether it's you or your student who is footing the bills. Don't fund their dating habits indefinitely. If you take the wheel, they will always want a chauffeur. How deep are your pockets? Before your student jumps to any expensive assumptions, have a budget review and let them know what you might offer, and what they will be expected to pay for.

Model It...

Here are some ideas:

- You might contribute $1 for the grade they are in ($9 for 9th grade, etc.) They need to come up

177

with the rest for each date. Be sure to set a **Solid Line** limit on the number of dates for which you will contribute this amount. **Dotted Line:** An exception might be made when a special event is endorsed by you but is too costly for the student to fund, i.e., science museum tickets.

- Reverse that concept–"As soon as you earn $9.00 (because you are in 9th grade), then I will give you an additional $15.00."

- Matching–"Whatever you earn towards the date, I will match." **Solid Line:** $200.00?! Set a top limit. Be careful with open-ended offers.

- If they have no money and no "real" job, create a list of "freedom chores" that give them the opportunity to "earn" the privilege to pay for a date. It certainly will make them think about whom they are spending money on. (And girls, this includes date clothing, hair, jewelry and shoes.) **Solid Line:** 60% of everything you earn needs to go into your college fund. **Dotted Line:** You can spend more on a Prom date than a regular date if you have saved up for it.

- Tip: Pay your student the same amount you would have to pay someone else for the jobs they do. If you pay them too much, they won't see the value... too little, you will de-motivate them to work for what they want.

- Consider a shift in thinking about gift giving: Instead of buying the GF or BF a wrappable gift, buy them an "event." Teach your kids how to give the gift of quality time spent together: two passes to the science center, two concert tickets, a day at the rock climbing wall, two hours of fishing… Encourage them to give "presence" instead of "presents." The benefits to this are two-fold: first, they achieve exactly what they should during dating (spending quality time together) and secondly, if they break up, there is nothing to return.

Ok. Now the toughest one: Spiritual and Moral boundaries. Not only are teens living for the moment ("I want the satisfaction right now!") they are struggling to become their own adult versions of themselves, so they are fighting against any perceived restraint. And never, at any time in their lives, have temptations been greater. They are bigger, stronger, smarter and more hormonal than they've ever been. If you come from a family of strong moral beliefs, you hope that by now you have instilled those values in your student over the course of their lives. But to enforce religious, spiritual, or moral boundaries, or as they might say, *impose* these on a teen, especially boundaries about whom they can date or what they are "allowed" to do, this is difficult for even the strongest parent.

Even if you have more liberal values, your definitions might not be the same as your teen's. The boundaries might be less clearly defined. You might think driving 65 in a 55 mph speed limit is okay, but they might stretch that to mean 95. In a later chapter we will discuss this more fully. For now I encourage you to have a discussion with your teen about your expectations to hedge the bet that they will choose wisely. And to reinforce to them that you believe that there *are* right and wrong choices.

Model It…

Define the expectations you have for your student based on your personal beliefs and morals. Make clear to your teen what you would like to see as they choose potential dates, but leave room for discussion as well. (Note to parents: Be very cautious about being close-minded in dealing with students who carry labels other than the ones you're used to. Make sure you honestly examine your own motives as you critically examine the motives of others.)

Solid Line: You might suggest that your student is not allowed to date someone from another religion (define what that means to you) or is lacking solid morals (give your student examples). ("Jorge comes over frequently to see Krystal but tells his parents he's at work.")

Dotted Line: If you meet a potential date, you feel they have a good set of morals, and their belief system does not conflict with yours, you would allow them to pursue a relationship with your student, even if their "religion" is different than your own. You may want to ask them to attend your place of worship and have an open, non-judgmental discussion about their beliefs.

Just like painting obvious lines on the road, laying out the boundaries right up front keeps confusion to a minimum. Tell your student and their date what you expect. Be clear, not vague. You can't enforce a blurry line. If either your student or the date is disregarding the boundaries set by you, talk about those limits right away and take appropriate action. The consequence for drifting over the line can be brutal.

Drive It Home...

DIA-LOG with your student during the next 10 hours logged.

How is your physical Solid Line?
Now that you have been on a few practice dates and are getting to know this person, how respectful are they of your personal and physical space?

Is there any area about which it is difficult to communicate when it comes to touch? Kissing, hugging, more?

Was permission asked and given to cross any physical boundaries?

Are you engaging in any activity that would not be ok for a five-year-old or your grandmother to witness?

How is your emotional Solid Line?
Describe how you feel when you are around the other student.

Have you experienced any negative feelings about yourself when the other student is present?

How safe do you feel with this person?

Describe how you will know when you are emotionally at risk with another person.

How is your financial Solid Line?
What is the most you have spent so far on one date?

In what way have you continued to budget and save for your future first before spending money on dating?

What dates have you had that are free of electronics? (No T.V., computer, video games…)

How much have you actually spent on birthday, Valentine's Day, the latest Hallmark holiday?

What ideas for events do you have to give as "gifts of time"?

What personal event is coming up that you need to save for? A football game? Lunch with friends?

How is your spiritual /moral Solid Line?
Would you feel comfortable inviting your date to go with you to your place of worship? Or go with their family?

How important is your belief system when it comes to compatibility?

Are you comfortable discussing your faith/morals with the other student?

What examples can you give of honesty? Integrity? Character? Trust?

Is there any pressure from either of you to change your values/morals/faith?

What things would you never be willing to do to compromise your morals/values/faith with this person or any other?

 **Road Trip...**

Student:
Examine this list of ways to keep your hands busy while on a date. Which ones are right (healthy distractions) and which are wrong (unhealthy temptations)? Add your own to the list.

- Hold the door open for your girlfriend
- Play cards
- Tie her bikini top

- Hold the water bottle for your boyfriend while he puts on his cleats
- Do dishes together
- Put suntan lotion on each other
- Hold hands
- Plant a tree
- Stand with your hands in your pockets
- Give each other a foot massage

Read Your Manual!

A little boy goes to his father and asks "Daddy, how was I born?"

The father answers, "Well, son, I guess one day you will need to find out anyway! Your mom and I first got together in a chat room on Yahoo. Then I set up a date via e-mail with your mom, and we met at a cyber-cafe. We sneaked into a secluded room, but neither one of us had a firewall. And, what do ya know, nine months later a little Pop-Up appeared that said... 'You've got Male!'"

Pull Over! I'm Driving!

I thought my mother was a conservative and cautious woman, until she took my sister and me for a spontaneous adventure ride on Wormwood Lane. My parents had a place up north, population 200 including road kill. One summer day on the way home from a trip to the one local grocery store, my mother decided to take the long way home, down scenic Wormwood Lane. She turned down this poorly-traveled dirt road (no more than a two-track with weeds as high as our axles), and we drove deeper into the woods. There had been heavy rains earlier and the washout was horrendous. There was evidence of a mudslide with grooves up to my pedal pushers. I looked over the edge of the abyss, and I wondered who had replaced my mother and was now driving this car. I wanted a refund on this amusement ride.

Our mother assured us that she knew what she was doing; she was "in control." But our little station wagon was not designed to handle off-roading, especially on Mt. Vesuvius. My mom chose a route that was not on the map, but to her it looked like fun. To us it looked like a scene from the movie "Earthquake." In reality, she should have pulled over and let me drive. *She* was way in over *our* heads.

> **➡ Pull over and let your common sense catch up.**

When I was director of a video dating service in California, there was one devastating mistake that people would make over and over again — they compromised their priorities. They tolerated behaviors in their "matches" that they said they would never accept in order to get someone they thought they wanted. Sound familiar? Your student said she would never date a guy who smoked… until she met Zach. "But he's so built, and he's captain of the soccer team." Yep. *And*, little missy, you just took the first step in settling for less. Welcome to Compromise-ville. Line forms to the right for Lost Dreams and Squandered Childhoods. There was a *reason* you set your standards high in the first place. Why are you compromising them now? Many teens will modify their own relationship rules based solely on W.I.I.F.M. "What's In It For Me." Sure his breath smells like an ashtray, but look at those pecs. (Wait 'til you see those pecs ripple with his smoker's hack. Now *that's* attractive.)

Let's look at this in driving terms. Right after teens get their license, they might drive with extreme caution, but as time goes on they relax and the "laws" become "flexible." Sure, the speed limit by the school is 25 miles per hour, but they have driven that street at 35 and no one stopped them. Your student just discovered a new "law." It's the law of "do it when no one is watching and you won't get caught." Stretching the law is not an activity limited to the teenage demographic. Next time you're on the freeway, see how many adults are driving over the speed limit. (It's easier to count how many aren't.) I know I'm guilty. Even the pastor of our church admits to speeding. So why don't we take the law seriously? *Because we keep getting away with it.* That's the "law of human nature." We draw the line in the sand instead of concrete. Nobody stopped us, nobody put up roadblocks, nobody took the keys away.

Kids practice this same flexible "law-making" in the dating arena. Imagine sending your sixteen-year-old to Europe for an unsupervised driving excursion during the German version of rush hour. How many teens are dating that way? How many teens are plowing down the Autobahn and there's no dating cop to say, "Whoa. Your skill level does meet the minimum standard to travel this particular freeway. Please step out of your vehicle."

➡ Teen Dating is W. I. I. F. M. = What's In It For Me?

Parents, this is the chapter where we come to a screeching halt and pull over for an inspection. Step out of the car— take a hard look at how well your student has done in this difficult dating arena so far and how well they will handle the challenges up ahead. Have they been making good choices? Any dents and dings along the way? Even if the road has been smooth and well-paved, it might be time for a front-end alignment before we speed back onto the dating highway.

In Michigan, Driver's Ed is divided into segments. Once a student completes Segment 1, the instructor decides if the teen can go on to Segment 2. The student must complete the classroom work and 50 hours of actual driving (including 10 hours at night). All the while, the instructor is watching for reasons to pass or fail your student. Not because they are cruel, harsh taskmasters, but because they have a very serious job to do — to keep our kids in one piece. (Although I'm not so sure about Mr. Moody, my driving instructor in the 70's. I think that his reason for living was to tell me how I couldn't parallel park if my bell-bottomed life depended on it.)

The driving teacher gives students a test they must pass to continue their education: *"You are given a knowledge test to determine how well you know traffic laws and safe driving practices. This test is administered by a qualified individual..."* Guess what? If you have given your student the big "thumbs up" to date, you have given them a passing grade. Your message was, "Sure honey, go ahead and keep dating. You haven't hit a wall yet. Have you? I've been a little pre-occupied with band boosters and the garden club." Since you are their primary dating observer, you must be the one to determine if they are in control and between the lines. If at anytime your student veers off course, it is your prerogative, no, your *obligation*, to take the wheel. If your student is dating poorly, it is time to take away his dating keys and give him some additional instruction.

Model It...

> Here is a crazy idea. Create a massive bumper sticker for your student driver's car that simply says "How's my driving?" and print your cell phone number on it. Can you say "accountability?"

By now, I hope the message is loud and clear that the most important thing parents can do to keep their kids safe while dating is to be involved. Talk to them, meet these dates, evaluate their successes and failures. Dry some tears. Answer some hard questions. You can't keep your kid "dating safe" if you practice the "whatever" style of parenting. The world is dying to get their hands on your student and teach them a thing or two. "Whatever" can get very expensive: child support, disease, or plain old heartbreak. You can't teach driving from the front porch. You can't parent from the couch.

> **Downshift into "let's just be friends" before you are emotionally "sold out."**

Don't wait. Be pro-active. Don't delay this inspection until after the crash. That's "airbag" parenting. Get in there now, early, while disaster is still preventable. The farther and faster these teens zoom into a relationship, the harder it will be for them to back up and back out. Are they dating someone with good character or are they parking in a dark secluded lot after curfew? Before your student is so deeply entrenched in a relationship that getting them out will require the Jaws of Life, intercede. Talk to your student. Before emotions override good sense.

Model It...

When you buy a car in Michigan, you have a "Three Day Right of Rescission." What this really means is that the dealership gives you three days to change your mind about your purchase. In that time, you can drive the car, inspect the car, get online reviews, ask your friends' opinions, and even shop for something better. You are not legally bound to keep the vehicle. It's only the test period. Let's relate this to dating: by now you have logged enough hours with your date that you have a pretty good idea what the pros and cons are so far. You might be pleasantly surprised, disappointed, desperate, or blown away. Bring out that old list from *Chapter 7: "The Perfect One"* that describes your perfect date. How close are you to what you set out to find? How would you describe your dating experience so far? What would you do differently if you could start from scratch? In what way do you feel your experience has been positive or negative?

As we've seen in driving, nothing replaces experience. Nothing will teach you the deep rules of the road like actually shifting into drive and moving forward. So now that your student has been steering down the dating road and logging some hours with a particular "friend," what has their experience been like? Have you shared your observations with your teen?

Have you been an attentive watcher from the passenger's seat or asleep with your headphones on? Do you recognize their good turns or bad, or are you yammering on about how tough your day has been without looking out the window to discover that your student has just driven you both into a very gritty part of town? Had you been paying attention all along, you would not have driven into The Under Belly of Society Hill — Population 3 and dwindling. Taking an active part in your teen's dating education is vital to their success.

> ## ➔ Is your teen following the world's dating curriculum or yours?

If you're going to claim "expertise" about the condition of a particular road, one would hope you would have traveled it before. If you're going to talk (or dare we think it— *give advice*) about someone your student is dating, you need information. What new ways have you found to interact with your student's new "friend"? Have you considered requesting them as a friend on their MySpace™ account?

Spending quality time with your student's new beau is crucial. How can you have any perspective if your only communication is "Hi, yeah, have her home by 11:00. Nice shirt." If you have not seriously interacted with this student, and your son or daughter has logged 60 hours with him or her, your ability to judge, or intervene, is nil. The sooner the better. After 60 logged hours your student might be flying down the dating highway turbo-charged with high-octane fuel, and how are you going to stop or even read the signs at that speed?

Have you made it your priority to spend the recommended five hours with this couple? That number is not completely random. It turns out that the average American spends five hours researching which car they will buy. Five hours *per car*. Five hours of time invested to insure someone's safety and security, whether it's driving… or dating.

Model It...

After you help your student buy their first car, after the test drive and checking under the hood and giving the tires a kick, you give your blessing, and off they go, never looking back! Hardly. Isn't it time to give it another good look? Take a peek under the hood to see if there are any rumblings. Take it for a little spin to see how it's handling and if you still feel it is safe for your baby.

In other words, invite the other student to come over for dinner. It doesn't have to be a Big Deal Meal, but it should be at a table with as many members of your family as you can fit. (Set up the folding chairs and the "kids" table.) Have your teen and their date help with setting the table, making a salad, serving the food — any activity that will inspire conversation and cooperation. This is your time to gauge the condition and performance of this pairing. How do they interact? How do they treat each other? How is the balance? After the meal, delegate jobs to the pair like clearing the table and doing the dishes. Have a conversation about the evening with your student after the date leaves.

By now, your student should know the predetermined number of hours they need to log with someone before the two of them become an "item," including those that should be spent with you. Hopefully, you took the time to meet the other student before they ever went out on their first "date" (kicked the tires and inspected the condition). That's just the beginning. Maybe you could agree that every third time together, the two students plan to spend a half hour hanging out with you before they go off on their own. Nothing formal, a snack in the kitchen, lemonade in the TV room, chitchat on the porch, you get the idea. The "first date jitters" have worn off and everybody's a bit more relaxed about whether every hair is in place and whether they used the correct salad fork.

> ➡ **Tailgating will only tick them off.
> Keep your distance.**

Personally, I encourage "co-dating," which simply means being around when they are. It means being an attentive passenger not a back seat driver. It means gathering sound bytes of their interactions. It does NOT mean hovering and being nosy. It does not mean that you invent excuses to wander into their space. Set the "cones" up early on. Have designated areas that they can sit that are "public." Front rooms not bedrooms. Balcony not basement. Basically, a room with a view... from your eyes to theirs. Be forewarned, some older teens may protest this (which is precisely why it's easier to start this "date training" when they are 10 years old versus when they are 16.) But be firm. Not keeping your eyes on your student driver's choices, can lead to brick walls. And that'll leave a mark.

Think of it this way. When your student buys their first car, they will need someone they trust to go with them to check it out. Another pair of eyes might see the dent in the bumper that your student missed. An experienced car owner will ask a question that would never occur to your teen. Here's a great example: my son saved up $3,000 to buy his first car at the age of seventeen. He test drove a 1993 Cadillac with 175,000 miles on it. The minute he sat in the driver's seat, he was in love. He's very tall, so the ample headroom and legroom tempted him beyond any other options. When we returned to the lot after the test drive, I simply asked the Seller if there were any known problems with the car. In his "plaid pants, beer belly and didn't shave this week" voice, he mumbled, "Yea, the air conditioning doesn't work." So I asked my son: "How would you feel about spending $3,000 to drive every day this summer to your intern job in wearing your business suit with the pond-sized sweat stains? Just to say you drove a Caddy?" He bought a Jeep instead.

When your student has lost his mind about getting some particular date, the "two heads are better than one" method might save you both some serious deodorant expense. Encourage them to ask their perfect date selection "who, what, when, where, how." Teach them to make their own decisions, to navigate with their own road maps. You are not trying to "hijack their agenda." This is not meant to be a battle. You are part of the support team. You are the instructor, the co-pilot, the primary observer. Teach them to think for themselves without automatically giving them a solution. Lead with questions, don't just give them answers.

Yes, they want to be independent thinkers, and you want to encourage that. But remember that as the parent, the Great Maker of Dating Mistakes, you have a vast source of wisdom to share with your teen. And all you want to do is help, not steer. Prove this to your teen by asking him or her: "If you were about to drive into a wall you didn't see, would you want me to tell you or let you learn the hard way?" It's the same with dating. They don't even see the wall. You're there to point.

> **If you don't like the way I drive... stay off the sidewalk.**

Guiding teens safely means upholding the rules. Rules aren't written simply to "keep us down" (although sometimes it hard to convince a teen who's chomping at the "I just want to have a good time" bit.) No, authorities and communities have created rules designed to keep us and others safe. When rules are broken, you pay the price; your driving privileges will be revoked (if you're fortunate and don't kill yourself first.) Even if you don't get caught breaking the law, no one wants to be in a car with you when you're out of control. The rules have changed over time as societies come to embrace new protections and reject obsolete ones. In dating, what are the consequences of breaking dating rules?

Model It...

Tell your student how some of the driving rules have changed since you were their age. (Like seat belts, speed limits, and your little brother riding in the "way back" of the station wagon, sometimes up in the back window of the boat called the family Impala. "Just hold him up there, kids. He'll be fine. Use two hands.") Open the discussion for ideas on how to adjust the dating rules you have agreed upon and work together on modifying those rules. For instance: maybe your student objects to having to watch movies with the lights on because it ruins picture quality. You state your concern that bad things happen in the dark and ask for a compromise. They then suggest watching the movie sitting up, no blankets in the Great Room next to the kitchen while you are cooking dinner. Problem solved... Their suggestions and subsequent discussion led to a mature solution.

So back to our routine check up: How is this new "couple" doing? Are they handling themselves well in this new relationship? Are they logging hours that really matter or are they just in "idle mode"? Your student can only gain knowledge and experience from driving, not idling in neutral. "Laura hangs out with Michael every day, but all they do is sit there." Relaxing on the front porch swing and not talking to each other is a privilege earned by old folks who have spent years together — not urgent, energetic teens in the throes of first blush. If your students are running out of things to do, engage them with questions both separately and together.

👪 Model It...

- **What is the most fun you two have had since you have been dating?**
- **Where do you come up with new ideas for things to do?**
- **What kinds of things do you have in common?**
- **What new things has your date introduced you to?**
- **Is there anything that makes it hard to enjoy your time together?**

Here is another common teen-dating pothole: fun fizzles when the focus turns to electronics. It is a rare couple that enjoys the same excessive amount of time in front of a box with a controller. When the only conversation comes from virtual characters named Commander Big Gun and Lieutenant Pea-shooter, someone is bound to get bored. Sitting on the couch month after month might indicate a stalled relationship.

➡ Wake up and smell the exhaust fumes!

Just because your teens aren't bored silly, doesn't necessarily mean they are on the right track. Are they demonstrating healthy dating habits? Is it obvious to others that your student knows whether they are going too fast or being careless? Are there restricted areas that your student has determined on their own to be off limits no matter what? Have they demonstrated the ability to recognize and follow signs? Do they know when they have crossed the line? ("Adam and Beth are the perfect couple. They got their tongues pierced together; they sneak out at night to smoke pot. Adam even took money from his mom to buy Beth a belly-button ring after he got her pregnant. He's so sweet!") Crashes happen fast. Do not procrastinate — save your student from a dating collision.

> **Your window of opportunity is much smaller than a garage door.**

To complete the inspection: Has your teen earned the privilege to keep dating? Have they gained a level of growth and maturity that is reflected in their level of responsible dating? They are probably discovering that it is much more difficult to get to the truth inside the person than it was to "fall" for their outward appearance. Ask your student to get out of the car, step back and take a good look at the whole package. The exterior – does it still seem shiny and pretty, or is it a little dinged up? (Does that just lend it character?) The interior— is it as clean as it was when you first began? What about the engine? Still running smoothly? And what about the driving record? How many serious infractions are there on the books? Put it all together – does this relationship pass inspection? Should they keep the relationship in gear?

Drive It Home...

DIA-LOG with your student during the next 10 hours logged:

Now that you've stepped back to examine the whole dater package, inside and out, which of the following dating methods will you allow your student to pursue? Check the appropriate box and discuss with your student:

1. Permission to IM, text, and email on their own:
   - Absolutely not
   - Only with adult supervision
   - I trust my student will use good judgment and does not need supervision
   - My student is too old to dictate to

2. Permission to have a MySpace™, Facebook™, or Blog on their own:
   - Absolutely not
   - Only with adult supervision
   - I trust my student will use good judgment and does not need supervision
   - My student is too old to dictate to

3. Permission to "group date":
   - Absolutely not
   - Only with adult supervision
   - I trust my student will use good judgment and does not need supervision
   - My student is too old to dictate to

4. Permission to date someone exclusively:
   - Absolutely not
   - Only with adult supervision
   - I trust my student will use good judgment and does not need supervision
   - My student is too old to dictate to

If you checked "absolutely not" for any of these four scenarios, are you "absolutely positive" they are not pursuing these options without your permission? Driving blind is dangerous. If you checked "my student is too old to dictate to," are you sure about this? Is there some bit of teenage leverage you can still wield to gain a bit of control for their sake? Cancel their text messaging? Make them charge their cell phones overnight in *your* bedroom?

Let your student "drive" this last section and share what they have learned so far. Do they show signs of maturity and levelheaded decision-making or are their wheels spinning in the dating mud? Do you feel compelled to increase your insurance coverage? Ask them to share some of what they have learned from logging hours and the "Dating-Log."

It's a great day when you finally get to take hold of the wheel and drive by yourself for the first time. This is a milestone for many reasons:

1. You have met the age requirement.
2. You have passed the driving test.
3. You have logged a ton of miles without a "crash and burn."

It is assumed at this point that your student can be trusted. So, ok, now give them back the keys. Get back in the passenger's seat — they they have more hours to log. Pay attention, there are some serious lessons ahead.

Road Trip...

Student:
What would happen if you woke up tomorrow morning and all the driving laws were lifted? All gone. Poof. Your alarm goes off and the guy on the radio is describing how every sheriff and police officer in the state turned in their badge the day before. During the night all the traffic signs were removed and the signals were darkened. You're free to drive however you want — any speed, any time, anywhere. Twelve miles per hour or 200, left side, right side, or on the sidewalk. Oh, and by the way, no more curfew.

Your job today is to take the neighbors' three-year-old to day care and then drive four hours to visit your grandparents.

Describe your concerns. _____

_____

What are your chances of arriving home unharmed? Might this convince you that the laws were originally made for your protection? This anarchy can describe the dating scene if you have no rules, no boundaries, and no limits. Establish your own personal set of dating "rules" and stay on course. Revise them as your experience and wisdom increase.

Read Your Manual!

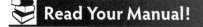

Some teenage friends were marveling at the scene of an accident where one of them had miraculously walked away from the accident without a scratch the night before.

"Wow, that was serious," said one.

"You totaled your car! What happened?" said another

The driver of the car said, "See that telephone pole?"

"Yeah."

"I didn't."

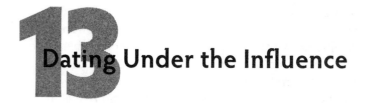

13 Dating Under the Influence

In January of 2008, a newspaper article stunned the nation. A mom from Iowa put her son's own vehicle up for sale because she found booze in his car. Yep, sold it right out from under him. Her name was Jane, and she was dubbed The Meanest Mom on the Planet.

There were plenty of heated debates around the water coolers the next day. Grown-ups everywhere took either the side of the poor victimized teen who had a cruel, twisted mother or the side of the mom, who, in one championship move, became a hero overnight.

Teens everywhere were, of course, outraged at this crazy mother. "She had no right to do that. Who does she think she is?" They could not conceive that maybe Jane thinks she is that misguided boy's responsible parent, the guardian of his safety, or something equally outlandish: his protector. The nerve of that woman. Somehow I don't picture Jane at her kitchen table with a latte and a legal pad writing the pros and cons of how people would feel about her if she sold her son's car. One thing was certain — that teen never had a chance to wrap *that* car around an old oak tree after a couple of keg-stands and a tequila shot. Instead, he lived to watch someone else drive away in his now famous "bar-on-wheels."

No matter where you stand on this story, you have to admit that particular mother took drastic measures to save her son's life. She drew the line in concrete, not sand. Sober concrete. She is not alone. We've all heard of MADD (Mothers Against Drunk Driving). MADD is an organization born from tragedy. And it's not just moms anymore rebelling and rising up. There are dads, brothers, sisters, aunts, uncles, and friends who have had life altering (or ending) moments because of a drunk driver. These outraged loved ones work very hard to prevent the next tragedy.

But the tragedies still pile up. People get behind the wheel, intoxicated, and create absolute chaos. Others get behind the wheel, just as intoxicated, but somehow squeak their way home. There are plenty of folks who have simply gotten lucky and gotten away with it— managed to weave their drunken selves home from the party or the bar, and this time, this one lucky instance, they swerved just in time to miss the lamppost, or the oncoming station wagon, or the pair of tottering grandmothers.

Many of the adults reading this book will know of someone who drove intoxicated and sideswiped a guardrail, but lived to tell of it. In fact, when I was in high school, it was a rare teen that did *not* have a drunk driving story to tell. The drinking age was only eighteen then. Most kids had possessed their licenses for less than two years. They would pour Mad Dog 20/20 into the depths of their inexperience, captain a two-ton boat through the dark streets with blurred vision, and pull into their parents' garage hoping the door was up. Some of those stories might even belong to you personally. Although choosing to share these experiences with your teen is your decision, at least use the wisdom that you gained. Would you want to stake your child's life on a precious sliver of luck or convince them that driving under the influence is about as wise as lighting a match at the gas pump?

➔ Is "high"way dating taking your student off course?

"Get off my back!" we used to shout at our parents or at The Man who was trying to keep us down (when they were really only trying to keep us safe and sober.) "Parents are just killjoys. Authority just ruins the fun." No, authority, The Man, would simply rather you not be blinded by alcohol when you drive inebriated passed his house. Near his children. Around his dog. You with the raging hormones and sense of immortality. Your parents like your face the way it is. Unbroken, jaw in one piece, all that orthodontia they paid for still intact. They like your face. They don't want to see it marbled with windshield scars. It isn't overly dramatic, it's overly possible.

"Gee, Mom, Graham's fraternity brothers drive home every Saturday night when they're wasted, and they make it home safe all the time. And they're in college." That must mean they're smart? No, honey, they're insane. Lucky maybe, but still insane. It's no smarter than being duct taped to a tree and letting your buddies throw knives at you. Most of the time they are going to miss. But every now and then...

I know, I know, teens feel oppressed and held down. And the minute they have a story that starts with, "We got so wasted, dude," and ends with "I don't know how we got home," they feel they've earned some kind of honorary badge that they must parade around on their key chains. The "I'm a Drunken Fool" amulet dangles right next to the "I Got My Girl Pregnant and Left Her for Someone New" medal. Oh, yeah. *That's* something to be proud of.

So how do you combat this mistaken impression that getting wasted "rules, Dude"? That Girls Gone Wild is not the way we select the next generation's leaders? Maybe take them downtown at night to walk among the homeless. Among those sad wanderers who have been chopped up, spit out, and rendered irrelevant by Lady Alcohol. Maybe you could stroll through the Neo-natal

Intensive Care Unit and coo at the two-pound crack babies who, if they're lucky enough to grow up, will be blind and asthmatic, destitute and dulled by what their mothers did to "have fun."

I had a conversation with a friend of mine about what happens to those partying people we knew in high school. Now that we're in (yikes!) middle age, we talked about how those decisions to live it up and get high affected our "real lives" today.

"Brian and I met in our early 20's. I fell for him the minute I met him. He was tall, had a beautiful smile, and was the funniest man I had ever met. We did everything together: dancing, hang gliding, scuba diving, road trips. He was adventurous— there was nothing he wouldn't try. We loved to party together and squeeze the most out of life, but almost always with a little added liquid courage. Or in his case, powdered courage. I chose Vodka Tonics to enhance our escapades; he chose cocaine. We'd get high and talk through the night about how blissful the rest of our lives would be. Getting high was our link to each other. It was what we did as a team. Underneath the buzz we might be dancing or discussing Van Gogh's left ear, but the cord that bound us together was getting high — a false simulation of the real world.

"After dating for two years we had a picture-perfect wedding. When I got pregnant, I slowed my partying way down, but Brian never stopped. His job was "stressful" and he needed his coke and his vodka for "tension." He was self-medicating. When he wasn't high he was depressed, moody, and lazy. He spent more time in his chair with his vices than he did with his family. We fought about the same things that brought us together — drinking and drugs. Brian was not fun, Brian did not take me dancing, Brian was gone. Who was this blob in the chair with the angry stare? Where was the beautiful man I married?

We divorced after six years of marriage. The real Brian had disappeared under a cloud of booze and cocaine.

The real Brian spiraled out of our lives in a cyclone of substance abuse. I look back now and realize, sadly, that maybe I never had the chance to know the real Brian, only the altered Brian."

There are no funny stories to tell in this chapter, only warnings to impart. We are so familiar with the cautions of driving under the influence, that it's practically a cultural staple. Old men can sit plastered on a front porch and shout, "Hey, kid. Don't drink and drive!" like it's the neighborhood slogan. It wouldn't surprise me if the latest kid's Sing-a-Long Road Trip CD contained such happy little hits as "Blow into this Tube, Tanya" and "Point Oh Eight, Point Oh Eight, Don't Let your Level Hit Point Oh Eight." We know we're not supposed to drink and drive. In drinking and dating, on the other hand, the rules are far less defined and nearly impossible to enforce.

Drinking and dating is a different kind of dangerous. Not only does it contain the driving component but dating under the influence can accelerate a person into a wall of heartache that hurts as much, if not more than concrete. The scars can be external as well as internal. Let's break it down into five parts: Fun, Fake, Feelings, Fysical, Fling. (Yes, yes, I know it's "physical" but that does not "phit" the alliteration.)

Does your date need a pill for a thrill?

Fun

I heard an expression several years ago, "I never met an alcoholic I didn't like." There might be a tiny bit of truth in that. We are drawn to the happy partier, the rejoicing "Whoo-hoo" guys. We like to join in when people are celebrating. Drinking can add something that's missing — confidence or wit. Or take away those undesirable traits we don't like — fear, tension, inhibitions and low self-esteem. Those built in fears and inhibitions are there for a reason — they keep us from dancing on balconies wearing beads and a cat mask. Drinking can be a lot of fun. At least in the beginning, until the depressive effects of alcohol set in and you wake up one morning wrapped in toilet paper stuffed in a grocery cart inside a men's locker room shower stall. Yeah, why don't you get *that* on tape? "Whoo-hoo."

Model It...

Okay, we're going to observe some actual folks under the influence. If your student is old enough, take him or her to a local restaurant or pub to see the "live" versions. If your student is under age, do your research on YouTube™. (The bar will have more of an impact, but you can navigate to a larger variety of venues on YouTube™. There will be no shortage of material in either place.)

Live:
Pretend you and your student are employers assessing the characters of people you might want to hire to drive your school bus. Find six individuals in the bar and study them for the next 30 minutes. Have your student write down the personality changes they observe in their potential bus driver. Record changes in behavior, voice, language. Do these people seem to get friendlier? More demanding? More touchy-feely? Write down how much fun everyone is having.

YouTube™:
(Search for these videos ahead of time without your student nearby to screen out inappropriate content.) Type in "bar scene videos" or "teens drinking" and select several examples of teens "reacting to alcohol." Use the same evaluation as above to study the behavior in the videos of a half dozen people.

> Now ask your teen if they would hire any of these people to assemble their automobiles, do their homework, or perform surgery on their dog. Ask if it would be okay to invite these same people over to live with you, permanently. Or, how would your teen feel if they saw you (the parent) in the video behaving this way?

Watching others getting high while staying sober yourself might seem "odd," but it can be a real eye opening experience. ("I can't believe Brianna actually jumped out the upstairs window after Ted. That's gonna mess up her volleyball career.") ("Dan is crazy. I don't know what he was on, but he ate at least four fish out of Doc Randall's aquarium. Wait until she gets back from her snorkeling vacation.)

We tend to tolerate, and even encourage each other to "loosen up" to have more fun. Do your kids only see adults enjoying themselves while they're under the influence? ("Mr. Hampton is hysterical after he has his evening Martini. He cracks the best jokes about his wife!") Make sure your student has an opportunity to witness adults having fun in sober circumstances: sliding down a zip line, mountain biking, or building a sand castle. What does your own student do to "live a little"? Boredom in a teen's life is deadly. Make sure you offer them healthy choices to excite their minds and bodies to keep them sober but stimulated. Consider giving them a pass to an indoor climbing wall as a gift instead of another video game. Here's a thought... go with them!

> ➲ **Enhanced experiences can lead to a thrilling spiral downward.**

Fake
Movies, TV, advertisements and all the glittery images of Hollywood can paint a seductive picture of drinking, drugs, and relationships. What is *less* than obvious to gullible teens is that the camera might show you 30 seconds of beauty ("Mmm, that's

a hot, manly man drinking that frosty, cold beer,") but once the camera shuts off Mr. Budly Studly is throwing up on his shoes.

In relationships, this dual image can also exist, especially if one of the people is under the influence. Maybe their new GF is shy and drinking helps her be more outgoing or confident. Maybe their BF is high strung and smoking mellows him out. But dating either of these individuals would not represent reality. Your student would be dating an altered version of their new "friend." An image, an un-real image. What happens when the buzz wears off? That real person will emerge and it might not be pretty.

So what's the big deal? Alcohol and drugs just make everything more fun, right? Not really. Because you wind up with way more than you bargained for: two personalities for the price of one. The problem is that you can't separate the two. Your student gets to date both at the same time... a split personality. They will end up trying to juggle two relationships at once — one medicated and one straight. Ask your student how they plan on breaking up with one and still keep the other. ("Jon is so much more patient after he has a bong hit in the morning, but he's a real grouch when he gets home from work.")

Drinking and drugs are a great way to artificially boost your personality. That drinker might very well be the life of the party. That stoner girl may become wildly romantic when she is altered. But it's a complete fake. The trouble for teens, and therefore the trouble for parents, is that teens do not see this as a bad thing. Neither do their friends. There seems to be little incentive to leave behind the personality they can only obtain by medicating. They *like* being altered. Or they are very attracted to someone who seems like the perfect companion after they've been using. To them it *is* the real thing. ("Andrew is so talkative when he does cocaine! Maybe if he did that in Mrs. Bevin's Science class, it wouldn't be so boring.") ("I love hanging out with Kayla when she's had a few. She's not nearly as negative about her life.")

Once an individual is clean and sober, reality sets in. Does your student recognize the stranger they have their arm around? Do they even "like" the person they thought they were "in love" with? What is the benefit to spending time with someone who doesn't even like himself unless he is altered? It's like cheating on a test. The temporary gain might feel worth it at the time but then you spend an eternity trying not to get caught.

> ➡ **What exactly is your date trying to make go away by medicating? You?**

The brutal fact is that drinking or doing drugs while you're dating is a flat out lie. It creates an image, a false, temporary image of a person or of a life that is impossible to maintain. There's a reason Marilyn Monroe was never photographed without her makeup.

In addition to keeping our teens safe from others who will act falsely or lie, let us not delude ourselves that our own teens will be 100% little angels and would never, ever use a prohibited substance. (Think back to your own growing up years.) A Breathalyzer is the ultimate lie detector. You can't follow your teen around with a Breathalyzer, but you can stay on top of things. At our house, if our kids come home when we are asleep, the rule is they have to come in and wake us up with a kiss on the cheek. Mints and gum don't cover up everything. If you suspect they are drinking or doing drugs, do a "random drug test." When your teen comes home, surprise them by getting out of bed and having a "lights on face to face" conversation about their evening for at least five minutes. Trust me, you'll know. And they'll remember.

Feelings
When you drive a car in a video game, you use the same controls as you do in a real car: a steering wheel, an accelerator, a brake. All the same parts are there except for the sense of pain or consequence when you hit the wall. You know you can have spectacular crashes and never feel a thing. This is not how real drivers learn to drive real cars. If this were a viable way of teaching kids how to drive, don't you think Driver's Ed instructors would have used this method by now? Yes. It is not until there is real

fear and real danger that we pay attention to the potential harm that comes our way. When we're sober, we have a natural instinct that sends up red flags to warn us of danger. When you drink, you might as well leave the red flags at home.

Model It...

Play a racecar video game with your student. Speed and take the turns too fast until you crash and burn. Push the button and restart the race. Do it again and again. Crash and get up, crash and get up. Talk about how nobody gets hurt, nobody dies. Discuss the delusion of this skewed reality. Help your teen understand that when you're under the influence of any mind altering substance, you lose your sense of reality. Danger becomes a distant concept. Crashing into a wall at 100 might actually seem like fun.

The reality is that being under the influence dulls the senses. There are reasons that there are laws against drinking and driving; you are unable to make good judgment calls. In fact, when you smash into that tree at 3:00 am, you might be so dulled against sensation that you don't feel a thing. Yet. Not until you wake up the next morning in traction with your leg in the air and your teeth in a glass.

> **Do you want to be the passenger in someone else's video game?**

Drinking will deaden real feelings. Altered people are artificial. They are just a simulation of themselves. It's like falling in love with a computer generated character. You miss out on all the real feelings, conversations, and decisions in this life. Unmedicated you are forced to work through problems instead of avoiding, stuffing, or masking the issues that will absolutely resurface once the temporary numbness has worn off. Like Novocain after a root canal. As painful as some of the feelings are, your student will have a better chance of coping if they learn to experience feelings and deal with them head on. There is really no good detour here.

Would you pour vodka in your gas tank?

Fysical

Many teens have no sense of their physical immortality. They are fearless, "bring it on" creatures with frontal lobes that are not fully developed that encourage them to bungee jump from train bridges in Mexico. They seem to have no concept that pouring alcohol into their own bodies is harmful. Yet, they would protect their precious vehicle from the same abuse.

Pouring alcohol in your fuel tank might sound ridiculous, but it makes a point. We know it would negatively impact the car. A drop or two may not make a huge difference, but an entire bottle could cause serious problems. Even though the working parts of a car are made of sturdy, high-grade metal, they are still too delicate to handle booze. The working parts of a teenager are even more sensitive and fragile, yet a teen would down a six-pack before he'd let you funnel one beer into his gas tank. A teen's perception of his mental and physical durability is twisted, especially when it comes to driving or dating under the influence. A teen might inflict damage to his or her body that they would never consider inflicting on their cars. How odd? How sad.

Model It...

Medicated Math
Grab your calculator for this one! Ask your student to do the math.

Here are the national IQ scale ranges for determining your intelligence level. There are several IQ Scales online. (This scoring table was found online by simply Googling "IQ Rating" and linking to www.wilderdom.com):

Over 140	Genius or almost genius
120–140	Very superior intelligence
110–119	Superior intelligence
90–109	Average or normal intelligence
80–89	Dullness
70–79	Borderline deficiency in intelligence
Under 70	Feeble-mindedness

Studies have shown that IQ drops as alcohol blood level increases. Assume you are average (just for this exercise). You have an IQ of 100. Each drink that you consume drops that number by 10%.

What happens to your IQ after two drinks? _____

After four? _____

After six? _____

The correct answer is = "My dream date is someone who is feeble-minded most of the time, but on good days is dull."

Fling

Having a relationship with someone who drinks or does drugs is kind of like having an affair. You may see the public life but there is a completely different life in private when no one is looking. The drug or beverage of choice is their secret love. It is what consumes their world, their mind. Their public life becomes just a façade covering up the desire for them to be somewhere else or more accurately, some*one* else. How long can anyone sustain that lifestyle? Seasoned adults (sometimes *well*-seasoned) have proven over and over again that it can't be done. How in the world can a teen be expected to manage? Why should a teen be expected to tolerate two people for the price of one? Managing any one relationship is a task that challenges even the most grounded and loving couples. Managing two at once is impossible. It won't be very long before trust is destroyed. Once trust erodes, the relationship is doomed, especially at this young age.

➡ **Dating someone who drinks or does drugs is like double dating... alone.**

Excessive drinking and drugs blended into any relationship adds a very disturbing element. The concern is not for adults who drink responsibly. Instead, let's take a very realistic look at how the mental and emotional alteration takes its toll on our students. After all, how many teens begin the evening by drinking one glass of Chardonnay and then switch to water? Very few. Unfortunately, especially in these young, experimental years, teens indulge "to excess" and get stuck there. When you try to develop a relationship with someone, and then have to include a *third* party (drugs and alcohol), the chance of success is very small. Not only is the trio more complicated, but it becomes extremely difficult for someone to abandon the very thing they based their relationship on and start fresh. Too frequently the person they fell in love with in the beginning is gone, caput, vanished. Now, the dynamics of the relationship are unfamiliar, unacceptable, and typically unwanted.

➡ **Mixing dating with drinking or drugs is like kissing on Novocain.**

When you're high, your perspective is distorted – about everything. Every aspect of a person (and a relationship) will be altered when you're under the influence: physical, spiritual, emotional, and financial. She's not really that cute. He's not really that funny.

When you're drunk and you're behind the wheel, you can't tell how far away that guardrail is. When you're in a relationship and you're drunk, you can't tell how far away your disaster is. But it is coming. Drinking and driving might land you in traffic court. Drinking and dating might land you in divorce court.

Getting high is a borrowed stimulation, and payback is brutal. Your student cannot afford the interest rate.

Kids have been warned about drinking and driving since they were old enough to read a billboard. Some ignore the warnings because of the thrill — because they are teens. They are immortal and untouchable. It's fun, it's risky, they might get caught… everything seems so attractive until they're on the floor of a jail cell worshiping a stainless steel Goddess without a lid.

Parents: do not let that stop you from trying to prevent this from happening. Love your kids enough to be the Meanest Mom on the Planet. You be Jane. You Jane. You tough. You want your kids alive and healthy.

🏠 Drive It Home…

DIA-LOG with your student during the next 10 hours logged.

Sober fun:
Name three compelling reasons not to drink or do drugs:

1. _____

2. _____

3. _____

There are lots of safe, healthy ways to get high on life. You want a rush? Go on a rollercoaster. There is no good excuse for having to be chemically altered to enjoy your life. Be the real thing. See the real sights. Explore the options in your own backyard. Get your thrills from things you can do in public that won't get you arrested. Go kayaking, take Samba dancing lessons, go to a college ball game. The choices are endless. You've got a lot of life ahead of you and if you can't think of anything fun to do, maybe you should park your car in the garage and buy yourself a La-Z-Boy™.

Road Trip...

Student:
Would you drive a car that had rat poison in the radiator? _____

Challenge yourself to find ways to have fun without drinking.

What three things do you do straight that you would classify as fun?

1. _____

2. _____

3. _____

Name three things you have seen adults do without drinking that you would consider fun.

1. _____

2 _____

3. _____

List at least five ideas for an exciting adventure without drinking or drugs. Be creative.

1. _____

2. _____

3. _____

4. _____

5. _____

 **Read Your Manual!**

My girlfriend told me we couldn't afford beer anymore and that I would have to quit.

Then I caught her spending $65.00 on makeup.

I asked her how come I had to give stuff up and she didn't?

She said she needed makeup to look pretty for me.

I told her that is what the beer was for.

I don't think she's coming back.

14 Emergencies and Hazards

I lived in Vail, Colorado, with some friends just after college. We skied hard every day until we were exhausted. One evening after a long day on the slopes, three friends and I were driving home, spent but happy, up a mountainside pass in my little Plymouth Horizon. We wound around the narrow mountain-carved lane, slightly numb and mesmerized by the moonlight, the stillness, and the slight dusting of snow settling on our car. Our vehicle was the only one on this mountain pass. On our right, the mountain sloped steeply upward. On our left, the embankment disappeared into an abyss. The gentle rolling effect of the road soothed our aching muscles and rhythmically hypnotized us.

Out of nowhere the road made a sharp turn to the right. I never saw it coming. The front left tire just peeked over the edge of the cliff. Time stopped just before gravity reached up to send the car plummeting to the bottom. Suddenly we were tumbling down the steep embankment, end over end, corner over corner. The world went oddly silent and in slow motion as windshield crystals floated like twinkling stars out into the glare of my headlights with each impact. Then the noise slammed back into our senses. Someone was screaming. Bonnie Raitt's red-headed blues blasted out of the 8-track player.

With a thud, I found myself sitting in the middle of the hill, outside the car, on the snow. I watched the car somersault the rest of the way to the bottom until there was frozen stillness. For a moment nothing moved. I looked down. I was in one, unbroken piece. I peered through the shattered glass window—my friends, still inside the car, were amazingly unharmed. In the hovering silence I realized that we were beyond lucky that the car landed on its tires and not its roof. None of us were hurt. I have no way to explain this, except to say that it was a miracle. Time and space returned to normal, the sights, the sounds, and the bruises flooded back in, but life was never the same after that. Tragic events have a way of changing your perspective even if you walk away uninjured.

This can be one of the hardest chapters for parents. Yes, bad things have been happening to kids since Eddie Haskell lured Wally out to the A&W to ogle the cashmere sweaters and drag race through town. Things had already gotten tougher for teens, but nothing like they are now. Life has become infinitely more dangerous for our kids.

"It's not like when you were a kid!" is one cry our children repeat that is actually true. Because a child's world has expanded from a twelve-mile radius to 12,000 miles, it is far more difficult to protect them. I can dial the dreaded Tech Support, and in 9 seconds I can be on hold with a human being in Bangalore, India. It can be just as quick for some psycho to reach out and touch your own child. Things are tougher for kids. The world is flatter. It is much easier to reach across it.

The dangers for our kids today have become almost incomprehensible. Drive-by shootings and car-jackings are routine, nightly news stories. Car bombings have moved from "the other side of the world" (where it didn't concern us) to "the lobby of the embassy" (where our own babies are being targeted like ducks at a carnival). The dangers in dating have become no less freaky: Kids who don't come back from Spring Break, kids who get secretly drugged by drops of mystery dope in their drinks, STD's that do more than raise blisters – they kill. What can begin as an innocent road trip can wind up as a headline: "Student's Car Plunges over the Cliff — Official Cause? They Were Teenagers."

> ## ➔ Is your student's call for help on speed dial?

The level of intensity of the "crimes" seems to have increased. In the 70's a Bad Boy might be a long-haired kid who smoked marijuana and listened to Pink Floyd. A Nasty Girl was someone who would kiss and tell. Now, a Bad Boy wears a polo shirt and sells Ecstasy or homemade GHB. (*Look this up if you don't know what it means; I had no idea there was a recipe online.) A Nasty Girl has a 3.9 grade point average and "protection" in her purse. *That's* who wants to date your children. And the reason this is so much more frightening is because one of the things that *hasn't* changed is human nature. Bad Boys and Nasty Girls have always been more seductive than a Goodie Two Shoes. There seems to be some invisible never-ending waiting line to get your heart broken, and then get back in the same line for more. That part hasn't changed. And many, many parents really have no idea what goes on at parties or on the Internet. That's why it's so important to be in the passenger's seat with sharp eyes to spot dangerous situations.

A bad relationship can be as devastating as a car wreck, except that you can pay someone to fix your car. It is far more difficult to patch up your child's broken heart. Or worse. Let's face it, with as many crazies as we've been exposed to in this Information Age, a broken heart might seem like the least of it. If your child is in a hazardous relationship, it is like driving without steering fluid. Nobody has any control over where they are headed. It won't matter if your hands are at ten and two if you're driving through the Fire Swamp dodging flame spurts and lightning sand.

🚶 Model It...

Think you are "anonymous" on the web? Google your name and see what comes up. Then Google your

> student's name. Cruise around on a MySpace™ or Facebook™ site with your student. Examine profiles of friends and acquaintances pointing out potentially hazardous situations. Show how much "innocent" information is actually given out and how easy it is to discover someone's true identity with very little effort. Example: "It says here on your friend's MySpace™ page that she goes by her initials K.M., but in her comments, someone calls her Katie. It also mentions the name of the local football team and where she will be on Friday night." Any amateur could contact her, lie to her, and pretend to be someone else. "Hey, my name is John and I LOVED the Cowboys when I went to your high school four years ago. Meet me in the bleachers, row 11 on Friday. I'll be wearing green shoes." It's just a small step to: "Green Shoe Bleacher Killer strikes again."

Banning our kids from MySpace™ or Facebook™ because it's dangerous is like forbidding them to drive on the freeway. Just because it's potentially dangerous, doesn't mean you don't use it; you just use it with caution. Let's teach kids to recognize the dangers and act accordingly, *especially when they are not within arms reach*. After all, how many kids behave differently just because no one is looking? It may take your son 15 minutes to drive you to the mall, but the return trip without you in the car only took him seven. It's not just while driving unsupervised where they behave differently. ("Alicia smokes her cigs out her bedroom window at night and covers the smell with the expensive perfume her parents bought her.") If someone else tempts your student to get involved in an activity that they know is wrong, a red flag should shoot up. There are flags that tell a race car driver his engine is on fire. Did your student misplace her flag? Check in the closet with the dirty clothes and candy wrappers.

Let's put on the flashers for a moment, look at some of the hazards of driving, and apply them to dating. The State Driver's Ed manual has specific instructions about where to park, where to drive (or not to drive) in order to remain as safe as possible. *"...be aware of your surroundings, especially who is around you, whether you are driving or leaving your vehicle in a parking lot."* It goes on to say that you should park in a *"well-lighted lot, close the windows, keep expensive goods out of sight and locked up, remove the keys and lock the vehicle. Consider buying an alarm."*

How much more true are those instructions for our precious teens? Did the thought of your student in that position make you cringe? Our culture fosters complacency and desensitization. These kids are easily conned by a sign that reads: "Cheap Parking. Leave your keys. We'll take care of everything." How much of a leap is it to imagine them being suckered into a party where the sign says: "Hot babes get in free. Leave your morals. We'll take care of everything." And it isn't just females who are targets. Young men can be just as victimized by predators.

> ➔ **Today, car jacking and auto theft are "equal opportunity employers."**

How do you keep your "expensive goods out of sight and locked up"? Do you keep your student locked up in the garage? Teens can be overly generous when giving out their personal data. Did you know Facebook™ includes both first and last names? Does your teen offer their cell phone numbers or addresses to perfect strangers? (If only the strangers were perfect—we wouldn't be discussing this.) How private is your student's MySpace™ page? Does anyone have the luxury of truly being "anonymous" in this new millennium? By the way, in the event of an actual car jacking, advise your teen: let them have the car. You can replace a Dodge Intrepid. You can't replace your beautiful baby.

Model It...

Call your kid's school to find out if they have had police officers come to talk about personal safety. (Chances are they have but it may not have made an impact. Your teen was probably busy texting the GF or BF about the new Whopper combo.) Why not take an evening to go down to the local jail and talk to an officer about what your teen should be doing to stay safe. Compile a list of questions about local arrests, current problems in law enforcement, personal security, and Internet issues. Many officers are happy to share their tales if it prevents them from having to look at one more innocent girl's face on a black and white crime scene photo. Allow a few of these undoubtedly horrible stories to hit home.

Whether your teen is driving or dating, there will plenty of close calls, but by logging quality hours they will learn to recognize hazards from a distance and steer clear of danger zones. You don't start out driving at an International Speedway. You don't start dating at a Rave party. The safest way to your destination is not always the fastest. Smart dating might mean driving "one more time around the mountain" with your student until you are *sure* they know the dangers by heart. Encourage your student to slow down and not be in a rush to get there. Enjoy the journey with eyes wide open.

Drive It Home...

DIA-LOG with your student during the next 10 hours logged...

Here are a few simple things your student dater can do while they're logging hours to stay out of hazardous situations. The following tips have been adapted from a Driver's Manual and applied to dating.

"Keep your vehicle in good working order."

Your student needs good, sound judgment. Drinking and drugs interfere with "good working order." If their judgment is impaired, their decisions will be also. "Stay alert" by staying straight.

Discuss the way each of these conditions/hazards affect your student and how they might occur. Driver's Ed instructors teach us to always have an escape route, not to ride or park too close to the car in front of us, not to get blocked in during rush hour traffic. Use role playing to explore the difficulty in finding an escape route when faced with each of these hazards. How will you stay in control…

> …when you are drinking?
> …when your date is drinking?
> …when you volunteer to take drugs?
> …if you are drugged without your
>   knowledge/consent?

"Have your vehicle id number chemically etched on the car window and main parts to help prevent your car from being stolen for parts."

This does not mean engraving a tattoo on their arm. It means that because of their own "chemical etching," their own DNA, you have a right to know where your kids are at all times. (And no, adopted children of the world, you do not get a free pass on this one either. You are just as innately bound to your adoptive parents as anyone else. Perhaps more so — you were *chosen* into the family.)

Your children are your personal responsibility. (Believe me, when your teen drives over the neighbor's dog, it will be to you, the parents, that the weeping owners carry "Fluffy" escorted by the police.) Not only do you have a right to know where they are at all times and to call and check on them, you can call their friends for an even higher level of security. ("Yo, Terry. Yes, this is Vinnie's mom. Again. Please put his about-to-be-grounded rear end on the phone.")

Program five of their friends' cell numbers into your phone. Get parents' numbers as well. If you call your student and don't buy the story they're telling, ask them to hand the phone over to an adult standing nearby. Then verify location and details.

Call a party in advance and thank the adults for having your child over and ask what your student can bring to share: pop, chips, cookies. You won't be just checking up on your kid, you will have a genuine reason to call. Be sure to follow through with the treats. Do not make an empty Oreo promise.

"Tell people your route and estimated time of arrival at your beginning and ending stops."

Turn signals and trip itineraries are for the benefit of others. It's about letting the people close to you know where you are going... every time. It is courteous communication, not an invasion of their privacy. (One of the ways to relate the fairness of this "rule" is to remind your student that they always know where you are. You can be reached at any time, and you will always be where you say you're going to be.) It's a two-way-street, not just "one way."

Make a rule that if their "address" changes, they must call and let someone know where they are going and with whom. (Even if they are only going next door.)

Do not accept these excuses:

> "My phone died."
> "I couldn't reach you."
> "You didn't pick up."
> "I told you yesterday."
> "The dog ate my phone."

"Stay alert for danger. Stay away from high-crime areas."

Consider this: is your teen more concerned with the safety of driving inside a big metal box with all the doors locked than they are about being alone in a dangerous place? Evaluate not just where your student is going but with whom they are going. Just because a place is crowded and well lit does not mean it is safe. Be a proactive parent, not a reactive parent. To avoid reactionary or "airbag" parenting, follow these three simple steps:

> Get names and locations ahead of time.
> Send them out with MapQuest™ directions or a GPS if necessary.
> If they have a cell phone, they should ALWAYS travel with a car charger, in the purse and glove compartment.

"Avoid the following behaviors: road rage, irresponsible drivers, tailgating, and giving angry gestures."

This one is pretty easy to read between the lines. Watch out for dangerously inexperienced or reckless drivers or daters. As your student grows immune to the consequences of violence and other extreme behaviors by witnessing it so often on TV, video games, and online, it becomes easier to dismiss the danger and consider it safe. Is your teen willing to risk giving a second chance to someone who has a volatile temper? Run, don't walk. No, better yet... floor it!

> Ask your teen about their new friend: "Tell me what you know about their reputation."
> Call other qualified and reliable parents to alleviate any doubts.

"Under extreme conditions, use controlled braking."

How well does your student handle extreme situations? Will they freeze or lock up the brakes and cause a collision? How will their "passenger" respond in difficult conditions? It's not a matter of *if* an extreme circumstance will pop up, it's a matter of *when*. We all know that steering your way out of a skid takes practice. Staying calm and using your head is the only way to get to safety. Does your student have a good, controlled, sensible head on his or her shoulders?

Go over expectations appropriate to where they are going:

> "If their parents aren't home when you get there, do not go inside and call me right away and offer another plan option."
> "If there is any drinking, I want you to call me and use our code and I will come get you." (Review *Chapter 4: "The Responsible Dater"* where you and your student created a "key phrase," a set of code words that instantly communicates extreme trouble.)

"When it's foggy, drive slowly."

Here it is: "When it's foggy, 'date' slowly." If your student has a hard time seeing what's ahead, maybe they need to slow down until the fog lifts. If the air is not clear enough to see both their passenger and their path, they may need to stop completely. Walls hurt even if you can't see them through the mist.

> ➡ **Dating requires miles and miles of good visibility.**

"If an oncoming vehicle is in your lane, look for an escape route."

When someone crosses the line and is coming straight at you, you had better already have planned how you're going to get out of the way—long before the impending crush of steel—or hearts. An exit strategy should be a part of every driving and dating experience. In the event your student dater gets into a tough spot, how will they be able to bail out safely without doing any harm or getting harmed? Always pack your own dating parachute.

🌲 Road Trip...

Student:
How does driving through a bad part of town at 2:00 am feel? (Let one little stone hit your windshield—you will immediately believe you're the victim of a drive-by shooting.) So should you take another route and avoid this area if possible? How is that any different from going

to a dark, unsupervised party until 2:00 in the morning? Is it any more dangerous? The unfortunate truth is, you're less likely to get car-jacked than you are to get assaulted at a "friend's" party.

Map out your escape route with specific actions for the following scenario:

You are riding home in the car with friends from a party. You are in the back seat. The driver stops at another friend's house and picks up a student who has been drinking. He climbs into the driver's seat before you can get out of the car. What will you do? _____

Reckless drivers endanger other people's lives. Reckless daters who lack a moral compass are just accidents waiting to happen. Why risk it?

Read Your Manual!

~

A guy and a girl are involved in a car accident and it's a bad one. Both of their cars are totally demolished but amazingly neither one is hurt. After they crawl out of their cars, the girl says, "So you're a guy, that's interesting. I'm a girl. Wow, just look at our cars! There's nothing left, but fortunately we are unhurt. This must be a sign from God that we should meet and be friends and live together in peace for the rest of our days." The guy replied," I agree with you completely. This must be a sign from God! The girl continued, "And look at this, here's another miracle. My car is completely demolished but this bottle of wine in the back seat didn't break. Surely God wants us to drink this wine and celebrate our destiny." Then she hands the bottle to the guy. The guy nods his head in agreement, opens it and takes a few very large swigs from the bottle and then hands it back to the girl. The girl takes the bottle, immediately puts the cap back on, and hands it back to the guy. The guy asks, "Aren't you having any?" The girl replies, "No. I think I'll just wait for the police..."

15 Night Vision and Visibility

When I attended Michigan State University I dated a guy... in Minnesota. "Absence makes the heart grow fonder," right? I was so crazy about him that I drove twelve hours to spend just five hours with him. It only took him four minutes to dump me. Great trip.

On the way home (sobbing, of course), I drove through one of the worst thunderstorms I had ever seen, or more accurately *not seen* — I could not see out of my car windows. The rain pelted the windshield like marbles. I could see only to the end of my hood. Already blurred by tears, my visibility was now equivalent to peering through a waterfall curtain. I should have pulled over and waited until I could see, but I just wanted to get back to my dorm and cry in my dry, cozy bed.

I flipped my windshield wipers up to "extreme" as they struggled to clear my view. Then on one partial swipe... they just stopped. Quit, never to clear again. I could hear my dad's voice in my head nagging me to replace the blades but I had been too cheap. I sure showed him. Now I was not only cheap, I was blind and stranded too.

Here's a revelation — you have to be able to see to drive. (Can you say "Duh?") You can't cover your windshield with bumper stickers, there's a legal limit to how dark you can tint your windows, you have to turn on your headlights... in short, you need good visibility. The state will measure you to make sure this is true. The manual says, *"You will be given a vision test to determine if your vision meets minimum standards."* If you can't see, you can't drive.

In dating, unfortunately, most teens cannot see anything beyond the exterior. Impaired vision might be the single largest impediment to healthy dating. Teens (and, frankly, most of us) tend to see only what we want to see. We look at a person and see only what fits into our scope of what we think we want, ignoring the obvious signs of trouble. ("Oh, I know he's married, but that's just a tiny detail we have to work out. We're so right for each other!") Do not let "Love is Blind" be a sticker on your bumper. Or your windshield.

Let's look at three different aspects of vision and how they can impair or improve dating: night vision, farsightedness, and hindsight.

Night vision is an interesting phenomenon. Many people, who can see well enough during the day to drive, have distinct difficulties at night. In fact when Old Man Johnson next door gets in his Oldsmobile after sundown to head out to the Bingo parlor, I initiate a call chain. Each caller barks just two words into his phone: "Johnson! Out!" then dials the next person the list. For the next 30 minutes, kids abandon the streets, dogs are yanked inside, and empty trash bins are pulled back up to the garage. Old Man Johnson, hunched over in his cardigan and fishing hat, can barely see over the dashboard. At night, he's like a directionally challenged pinball, relentless but fortunately slow, that zigzags through town at the speed of granite settling. This is one guy who should only drive during the daylight hours.

> **"Dark and secret places" are the favorite dating destinations.**

Dates most often occur at night. After all, during the day we're working or going to school, so by default the sun tends to be down when two people are logging their dating hours. This darkness lends itself very nicely to goo-goo eyes and romance. ("Oh, Austin, I love the way the moon brightens your smile.") ("Lydia, the starlight reflecting off your hair looks like heaven.") But remember, the sun will come up. It has happened every day so far, it will probably happen again tomorrow. And kids need to see beyond those moonlit moments and expose their relationships (and flaws) to the light. Those midnight meetings, with all their imperfections hidden (and parents nowhere to be found), can create a false sense of intimacy for teens. Flickering candles, moonlight, or the blue glow of the TV can jump-start their starved-for-romance brains (and bodies) into behaviors that feel so adult, but are just too premature.

By this time in a relationship, your student has hopefully logged 30 or more hours getting to know someone. At this point one of two things will usually happen:

1. The newness is beginning to wear off (yawn)
2. The chemistry is almost unbearable (fireworks)

In either case, the tendency may be to turn the relationship into a physical one. I mean let's face it, if you're bored, maybe a good roll in the hay will liven things up. And if you're not bored, if you are in fact aflame with desire, you might be thinking about heading to that same hay-strewn barn to keep the fire burning. Bad idea. Sexual intimacy should be a long way off for these kids, hopefully accompanied by a marriage license, forty birthdays, and a nine year engagement.

The answer for both dating dilemmas is brightly lit, visible, healthy adventures. Keep away from dark barns altogether. You don't need gasoline and a straw bale to light the fire. Watch your teens for signs of boredom. Sometimes this might simply be a lack of imagination on their part. Maybe all they can come up with is to go to the mall, again. Make some new suggestions for safe and highly visible outings that will stimulate their brains and their relationship in a healthy way. Stay out of dark and deserted places where other watchful eyes are scarce and hormones can run rampant.

If your teen is truly bored with his GF, imagine how he will feel in another six months. If all they have going on between them is a physical attraction (but she's so pretty), how long will this last? How long can you simply sit inside the flashy showroom car in your driveway and never go anywhere?

Model It...

Tell Your Male Student: Your principal's drop dead gorgeous teen daughter named Karina is coming to stay with us for a week. I am putting you in charge of making sure she has a great time while she's here. I will trust you to find things to do that are fun and appropriate. Oh, by the way... she's highly allergic to electronics. Name five ways you might entertain her at night.

Tell Your Female Student: Your principal's drop dead gorgeous teen son named Ken is coming to stay with us for a week. I am putting you in charge of making sure he has a great time while he's here. I will trust you to find things to do that are fun and appropriate. Oh, by the way... he's highly allergic to electronics. Name five ways you might entertain him at night.

> **Don't blame missing your exit on the full moon.**

Farsightedness. Parents, your kids have been going on dates for a while now, and perhaps they really are falling for their new girlfriend or boyfriend. Let's help them clear away the mist from their eyes and not lose sight of their own dreams and goals. Remember, this is a turning point in the lives of many teens.

Where is your teen headed? So many kids at the end of high school will go on to college or move out to pursue some other "What do you want to be when you grow up?" avenue. This is it — these are the "growing up" years, and their relationship with another student will either help them or hinder them in reaching their desired destination. ("Marcia wants to go to college to be a veterinarian, but her boyfriend Geoff is allergic to cats.") ("Aaron is joining the Army when he gets out of school, and Trish is excited to travel with him to all those exotic places.")

You need to have your eyes wide open when choosing a mate. Love is blinding. How many people were aware of their partner's obvious character flaws (choose one: alcoholic, aggressive nature, lazy) and married them anyway? Five years into the marriage both people are miserable because they thought they could change the other person. They thought it would get better, that whatever was wrong would just go away, that they could blow some magic dust on the problem and it would disappear. "But we love each other. (*Sigh, blow magic dust.*)" As parents, we've driven that road and we know better. Relationships are disintegrating all around us. The house of cards will come tumbling down and its echo will sound like: "I-should-have-seen-it-coming-coming-coming." Choosing to join the Army and travel the world is not at all a character flaw, but it might provoke incompatibility if the other person never wants to leave their hometown.

One of the most valuable instructions I was given when I was learning to drive (by my mother, no less), was to drive "further on down the road." This means that when you drive, you should focus your eyes beyond the few feet directly in front of you. Look down the highway at the upcoming twists and turns, so you can anticipate them. By the time you get to the next road condition (say there's a line of brake lights merging into one lane up ahead), you will have already adjusted your steering wheel and your accelerator — smoothly and without slamming everyone in the car against their doors. If you only focus on the nose of your car and your fancy hood ornament, you spend all your time making constant, instantaneous corrections. You'll have the stress level of an air traffic controller and you'll *still* hit the mailbox. Focusing "down the road" will help your vision (and your passengers) tremendously. You'll be able to turn the corner without ending up in someone's front yard. Eyes up.

When we look at the people in our lives, we need to gauge compatibility not just for right now, but for the future as well. First look at who they are now: does he study hard, take regular baths, say please and thank you? Is she demanding, pouty, and spoiled rotten? Then, look "further down the road" at the potential. Who might this person become? Will he be a reliable companion and provider for his family? Will she be a relentless gold-digger? Look at the goals they have set for themselves. Does your boyfriend want to be a missionary in the Congo? Do you want to be a pampered picket-fence wife? Your vision needs to be 20/20 when you drive. When you date it needs to be just as clear. Look plainly and without prejudice at yourself and at your potential dates to determine if the relationship has a long-term chance.

> ➡ **When you say you are "seeing" someone, do you mean it?**

When you're shopping for a car, you don't always see the flaws as you swoon over its luxurious shape. "What do you mean the bumper is a different shade of green? Just look at those curves." "It only gets 10 miles to the gallon, Ted. How are you going to commute to college in this boat?" "But it has spinning rims, Bob. *Spinning rims!*" Examine your investment, whether it's a long-term relationship or a car, for whether it will be a good fit for any length of time. If your student knows she's going to move to California after she graduates, does it make sense to become attached to a boyfriend now, one whose heart will be broken when she leaves? Consider the lease. These kids *can* just go on casual dates if they are focused on their future. They don't have to commit to being mates for life. They're not swans. If this is a short-term commitment, you should be very up-front about that.

If you are leasing, you need to say so. *Do not* toy with someone's heart. You wouldn't want it done to you.

Model It...

While you are in the car with your teen chauffeuring them somewhere (again), take a different route than you normally would, one that's longer or has more stop-and-go traffic. After some time, pull over and have a chat about how easy it is to lose sight of a destination and veer off course unless you really are paying attention to your goal. Discuss which route made more sense. Not all roads lead to the same place. Help your student make a list of where they think they want to go in life (we know that may change) and how relationships will help or hinder that goal.

> ➡ **Is your dating GPS pre-programmed with a specific destination?**

So put on your Coke-bottle glasses to reveal the potholes in the road that will impede your student's progress. Getting to the finish line is hard enough for young people. Why drive the hardest and most difficult road when you could avoid it?

Most people do not undergo drastic personality improvements. Very few adults who "suffer" from a character "flaw" ever experience a major personality overhaul. However, before you inundate my website with stories of the exception, not the rule, hear me out. Yes, some people may embrace a conversion in their lives, and incorporate large-scoped changes into their personality, usually on the heels of a life-altering event or experience. But, you cannot depend on a change like that to occur. Most of us are who we are, are who we are, are who we are. Couch potatoes rarely leap up off the couch one day in a blaze of blinding light and say, "Today is the day I stop wasting my life. From this day forth I will invent a cure for cancer made from Cheetos." That's a half-baked (or maybe twice-baked) idea. Rarely do vain girlie-girls toss their lipstick to one side and shout, "What have I been doing with all these shoes? I will start a non-profit organization to collect pumps for the poor!" Maybe she *has* been "sole-searching" but guys, if all your dates only consist of taking her shoe shopping, you might want to look for a new GF while you are at the mall. Follow the map to Girlfriends R Us.

No, people are who they are. Examine whether the relationship "fits." Are you bored or comfortable? It's all right to be comfy; it's not all right to get complacent. Do the two little love-doves create fun, intentional time together or do they waste their hours hanging out in front of the idiot box?

> ➡ **If you're bored, then maybe you're the one who's boring.**

Around here, if you dare to say "I'm bored" out loud, then you better be prepared to hear someone in this house tell you to *find* something to do. Make it happen. Go outside and count garden rocks. Make music on the mailbox. Sort those thousands of abandoned LEGOS. Color with crayons — you can practice staying inside the lines. Boredom is internal. Get over it.

On the other hand, comfortable is underrated. How many of us have a pair of old shoes that we cannot get rid of? My kids cringe when I pick them up after band practice wearing my stained and spotted tennis shoes. But, man I wouldn't trade them in for all the shoes in Imelda Marcos' closet. I'm not even sure I'd give them to Pumps for the Poor.

My car is the same way. I own a minivan. Boring, right? Maybe. But why do the car companies sell so many every year? Perhaps because working moms like me chauffeur band kids, haul groceries for entire soccer teams, and drag home fertilizer for the lawn. I need what this boring van has to offer: disappearing seats (to make space for emergency band equipment), a built-in DVD player (to play reruns of Gilligan's Island), and automatic sliding doors (when I can't come to a complete stop when I'm dropping off kids. "I'm gonna slow down — one, two, three — jump!") Millions of families with children find great value in this boring box with the vinyl, gum resistant fabric. Is it my dream car? Not by a long shot. But I knew that owning a Mustang convertible with two small children would not make sense. The mini-van fits me. It's boring AND comfortable.

This brings us to the coveted position of hindsight. Oh, how I wish I knew then...

Hindsight. Been there, done that. How those words can inflame a teenager, especially coming from you, the wise parent. First of all, they don't believe that you've ever done anything remotely cool or wild or "out there," and second, even if you have, "You can't possibly know how it feels to be me!" Have you ever been impaled by that crumpling cry from your hormonal daughter? Or jumped at the slam of a door as your son stomps into his bedroom and turns up his iPod™? We *do* know how they feel. We *have* been there, we *have* done that. You may have to show them that you were once young and stupid by pulling out old photos of yourself with teased hair and parachute pants. Perhaps you even dated a high school drop out named Jethro and have the photos from the barn dance to prove it, in matching overalls.

Let's face it, adults naturally have some significant mileage on them.

You would like to share what you've learned about relationships to keep your teens away from as much heartache as you possibly can. That's how you've been teaching them to drive — you keep them on the road and out of the ditch using the benefit of your experience. Apply that experience to dating. Your crinkly old viewpoint just might help them see themselves or a potential date in a new way. It might even make you seem more human.

(Parents are human?) You don't have to share whole entire stories, but the Cliff's notes of some might be of value.

Model It...

Talk about your dreams and aspirations when you were a teen and how dating played a part in where you are today. Both good and bad relationships got you to where you are now. Share some of your insights and what you learned along the way. How did dating affect your school work? Your family life? Your friendships? Your plans for the future? Stay away from blame; model responsibility and ownership of your choices instead!

To get the benefit of hindsight, you don't have to look back all that far. You don't have to look back to the Ice Age to find out what yesterday's weather was. Seeing what your date has done in the recent past can give you insight into how they will behave in the future. You would do the same for a car you're going to buy. Or sell in the future. When a new car comes off the assembly line, it is in the best condition it will ever be in. The leather interior will never smell the same, the shine will never be as polished, and the engine will never purr like it does as you drive it home from the dealership. How you treat it from that day forward will dictate how well it will run for you and how much it will be worth when you go to sell it. If you keep it clean, change the oil, and keep it tuned, it may give you years and years of good service. If you are lazy, careless, and abusive to your car, after a while it will stink, it will run poorly, and get poor gas mileage. In short, you will probably want to dump it.

The same is true with our teens. Does your teen treat his body like a well-kept machine: eat right, get plenty of sleep, exercise? Do they pour intelligent works into their brains or dump sludge and oily bits of trash talk? Do they treat other people with respect and dignity or are they small humans with small, mean egos and no compassion for suffering? Hindsight — have them look at what their behavior reveals about themselves and their dates for the past few years they've been on the planet. It will give them some insight into how well, and for how long, their relationship will run and whether they will get good mileage together.

If you could go back in time and undo some of those decisions you made in high school, you probably would. Some of the silliest little things have a way of turning ugly if we have no foresight about what they will do to our future. If your teen polled only his friends at school, they might vote overwhelmingly in favor of him getting a dragon tattooed in his skin. If he asked his family and church members instead, do you think the outcome would be the same? This is not a comment about whether tattoos are okay; it is simply a reflection that we need to examine (more than superficially) the choices we make that will affect us forever. Personally, I've had a rainbow of hair colors (including eggplant) and styles with names like "The Quiff." Bruce broke up with me over that one.

> ### ➡ Will your lip ring get in the way when you take out your dentures?

Adults know that what is cute today is not always so cute when you're 60. Here is my parenting example: I told my kids when they were little that they had complete fashion freedom. They could wear anything they wanted. They could even style their hair and makeup in any shape or color they desired. The only catch was this: if I didn't like it, I would show up at school during lunch hour looking the exact same way. Now *there's* a vision. Picture a mom wearing the miniskirt and fishnets her teenage daughter just bought. Imagine a dad sporting a green Mohawk to work. Imagine what that dragon tattoo would look like on my saggy arm. Yuk. After a few years, it will look more like a Basset Hound.

Hair and makeup are temporary changes (thank heavens!) that grow out and are relatively harmless. But what about more permanent choices? Would it be ridiculous for your son to go with Grandma to have her belly button pierced? Would it be ok with your student if you got fired for smoking pot? Can Amanda go to college pregnant? Will Blake be able to get his degree online from prison? Driving laws are the same for 25-year-olds as they are for 56-year-olds. Driving style on the other hand is acceptable within the law. Yes, you can have your own style, but you'd better make wise choices. You can (legally) drive an entire journey in the left-hand lane of the freeway at exactly the speed limit if that is your style. It is within the law. (However, would you please notify me where you'll be when you do this? I'd like to avoid that particular strip of Frustration Freeway.) But if you're dating someone who rides on your passenger side who really enjoys the colorful gestures of all the people passing you on the right, it might be a match made in heaven.

Good vision. Driving at night, looking forward, and looking back is as crucial for teens while they're dating as it is when they're driving. When you take the vision portion of the driving test, if you cannot see the letters on the eye chart, the state makes you wear corrective lenses. So, parents, guess what — you *are* the Corrective Lenses of Dating. You get to clean off the Windshield of Obscured Perception, flip on the Bright Lights of Clarity, and focus the Lens of Hey-What's-That-Character-Flaw so that your student can see the true nature of the road in front of them. Whether it's lined with potholes or promise, it is undoubtedly easier to travel if you can see it. The time to coach them is now. Have the foresight to know that they will someday, in hindsight, thank you. And hopefully neither one of you will have a saggy, morphing dragon tattoo on your arm.

🏠 Drive It Home...

DIA-LOG with your student during the next 10 hours logged...

Anything you alter on your car changes its value, for better or for worse. Look into the future of the following examples. Which of the following changes do you think would "add value" to these vehicles?

- Spinning rims on a rusted out VW Bug
- Lifts on a brand new truck
- New leather seats in a car with 167,000 miles on it
- Replace the engine on a Honda with 50,000 miles on it
- New paint for a 1985 Mercedes
- Rotate the tires after 3,000 miles

> ➡ **Whatever you do to change who you are, will change who you attract.**

Which of the following changes would "add value" to your own future?

- Staying in shape
- Smoking pot
- Working hard for your grades
- Spending countless hours watching T.V.
- Wearing clothes that are appropriate
- Drinking with friends
- Body piercing

Go over this same list, this time asking those questions about parents or guardians. What changes could an adult have made when he or she was a kid that might have changed his or her present condition?

Road Trip...

Student:

I want to sell my minivan. I have determined it is worth $20,000 in its current condition. There are 30 minivans listed in the newspaper with the same basic description, and there are 500 people searching for mini-vans in my town.

Before I put an ad in the classifieds, I decide to paint bright orange flames on the side of my van and install a turbo charged V-8 engine.

- Out of 500 potential buyers, how many are interested now?_____
- Has the $20,000 value change? _____ New perceived value?_____
- Have I just made a shortsighted decision that minimizes long-term marketability? _____
- What if I had not changed the oil, tires, or brake pads in the last five years? _____
- How does neglect affect the value of the mini-van? _____
- How many people are in your school? _____
- Assume ½ are of the opposite sex meaning that there are a total of _____ potential dates.
- If you got your tongue pierced, how would that number change? _____
- What about your interior features? Do you always have to have the last word in a debate? Does your tongue throw out piercing words? How does this alter your resale value? _____

- Students, do you get a tattoo because you feel like it today or because your grandkids will like it?

  _____

- What if you get suspended for cheating on exams? How will that affect your future marketability?

  _____

Make a list of the things you have done that increase or decrease your personal worth:

Appearance:
　　Increase: _____ Decrease: _____

Reputation:
　　Increase: _____ Decrease: _____

Future Goals:
　　Increase: _____ Decrease: _____

Changes to your marketability, especially negative marks against your reputation, may last years beyond your (long-gone) high school sweetheart. What are you doing to improve your long-term marketability so that other people's vision of you is crystal clear? _____

Read Your Manual!

~

"Your goals are the road maps that guide you and show you what is possible for your life."

—Les Brown

"You can close your eyes to the things you do not want to see, but you cannot close your heart to the things you do not want to feel."

—Author Unknown

"Map out your future — but do it in pencil. The road ahead is as long as you make it. Make it worth the trip."

—Jon Bon Jovi

~

"The magic of first love
is our ignorance
that it can never end."

~Benjamin Disraeli

# Passing the Test

We went on a family vacation to San Diego and rented a car for the trip. All the rentals came equipped with a GPS. Yes! No more upside-down map and origami lessons for us. Just punch in an address and "the box" would tell us where to go next — in a serene, female voice. The voice sounds like she's doing yoga, like she's meditating on a beach at sunrise with no worries. "Turn left." "Turn right ahead." "Isn't life grand. Om." My daughter named the box "Dreama" because of her "sleepy-dreamy-sultry" voice. It was very soothing — until you messed up. When my husband missed a turn, "Dreama" would calmly point out his flaw by saying "Off route," followed by, "Please make a U-turn." This was the Dreama Sequence.

She would repeat this every few seconds until you were back on course. Eventually, we started to mimic her by making up new things for her to say. One time we needed to turn into a neighborhood that was blocked by construction. Dreama couldn't adjust. She kept taking us in big circles and couldn't guide us to where we needed to go. Around and around we went. "Off route, please make a U-turn. Off route, please make a U-turn." (Dreama was unaware of "quirks" like accidents and detours. She only knew her pre-programmed route.) Finally, in his best "Dreama" voice, our son chanted: "You stupid fool, where did you learn to drive. Pull over and let someone else try."

Your student is no "stupid fool." He has been itching to get out there on his own and date by himself. To prove to you, to his girl, to his buddies, and to himself, that he has been paying attention to all the instructions and passed all the mini-tests along the way. He has become familiar with the signs, hazards, weather, and laws that tell him how to behave as the pilot of this vehicle. He has learned how to stay safe, to have fun, to be compassionate, and even to talk to his date's parents. He has studied the emotional maps in case his GPS (Guy or Girl Prospecting System) fails. He is using his good common sense as a backup in case of total power failure.

It's time to graduate.

> ## ➥ There is no portable mapping device for "Global Positioning Singles."

You're at Dave's Deep Discount Driving School. You're in the lobby drinking Dave's Deep Discount coffee watching out the window for your son to return from his final road test. In pulls your son with a triumphant smile on his face. In his elation he whips into a parking spot much too quickly and nearly drives through the plate glass into your euphoric lap. Discount Dave, both bored and edgy in the passenger's seat, jiggles his clipboard and shoots a caffeinated glare at your son, like, "Hey, don't blow it now, pal." And he doesn't. Your son slams it into park, leaps from the car, forgetting even to turn it off and rushes you with a hug. "So I guess you passed," you say into his unwashed hair, with a mixture of delight and absolute mortification.

Oh my, oh my, you agonize to yourself. My student has passed the driving test. So this means, let me get this straight, that he gets to drive around town without me. Without me in the passenger's seat offering such helpful hints as, "You know, that Stop sign is more than just a good idea." Or, "You could drive around this blue-haired grandma, but that Mack truck might have something loud to say about it." Without me in the passenger's seat saying, "Off route, please make a U-turn."

This is what you've been hoping for, right? You get out from under all those chauffeuring duties. No more scrambling home early from work, changing into sweat pants and eating Pop-tarts in the car just to get your student from dance class to her soccer game on time. Now she gets to drive herself.

The same is true for dating. These kids are out there, dating, driving around, without us to keep them on the right road. Your student will, of course, rely on autopilot for much of his dating pursuits, but every step of the way even his autopilot choices have been informed by your constant direction and instruction. Like Artificial Intelligence — they develop and evolve an amazing set of new "rules" based on the inference of the things you've told them. Their own inner voices tend to be excitable and tinged with fear, doubt, and hormones. These inner voices want to break and squeak (in males) and rise and squeal (in females) and therefore communicate somewhat garbled instructions to their immature brains. We have tried to instill in them a decent sense of direction. When they do get lost, hopefully the voice in their head that tells them how to get back on course sounds a lot like the voice of their gentle parent. "Off route. I don't think so, sweetie. Don't go there."

Getting lost is only one of the frustrations of driving. Breaking down is even worse. Fortunately, one of the greatest bonus items that come with every new car is an owner's manual. Not necessarily a literary work of art, but informative nonetheless. This little book of treasures tells you how your particular vehicle operates. Every car may have an oil filter, but yours has exact specifications that you need to know when it's time to replace it. (Mine should have come with a warning: you will need to take out a government-backed loan to replace a lifetime of oil filters. They are as precious as gold and will need to be replaced every time you think about it. There. Now I have to do it again.)

Let's take a breakdown as simple as a flat tire. (Simple? In a Michigan winter?) The first time you have to change a flat, it can be as daunting as heart surgery. Where is the jack? *What* is the jack? Having the manual handy can dictate how this crisis plays out. Have manual? Can do. Don't have manual? I hope you have a pumpkin coach and four white horses you can call, Princess. Once you've replaced a couple of flat tires, you may not need to refer to the manual anymore… until the next car. In the next car, the jack might be under the hood, not in the trunk. You might find you use the manual far more than you expected. Cars are complicated. Just knowing how to drive is not of much value when you are stuck by the side of the road with a flattened tire and deflated self-image.

> **Would you throw out the manual for your second car because you knew how to change the tire on your first car?**

Cars break down. Knowing how to fix them (or at least find someone who can) is crucial to remaining mobile. In dating, unfortunately, people break up. The models are different, the parts might be in different locations, but the "why" is usually the same: someone wants out. Neil Sedaka was right: Breaking up really is hard to do, and it is nearly inevitable. How many of were crushed, brokenhearted by our 5th grade sweetheart who stole a kiss behind the jungle gym? The more time your student logs before they date and commit to someone, the better chance they have of not getting burned. Even the safest cars in the world have collisions. Your teen can't always avoid a wreck but they can limit the damage and recover faster if they try to follow some common sense dating guidelines.

Here are some tips for breaking up:
- Face to Face — as long as there is no abuse involved, break up in person. IM'ing, writing a letter, or "phoning it in" is immature (and cowardly). If you

are old enough to date in person, you are required to break up in person.

- Give back anything that was not a gift. If it was a gift, it is yours to keep. Anything else that does not belong to you (t-shirts, CD's, his mother's Tupperware) needs to be returned within a week.

- Always meet in a neutral public place. You may not know what the reaction will be, so keep it brief, and be sure there are lots of people around. Girls, make sure you have someone to leave with afterward in case it gets messy. This does mean that you bust the guy where everyone can hear. You are not trying to embarrass him. Select a private corner of McDonald's. Maybe over by the Play Place where all the surfaces are foam-padded.

- Let your parents know you are breaking up and where and when it will occur.

- Break up as early in the day as possible. This gives the other person daylight hours to get used to the idea. Everything is magnified in the nighttime. Hurting someone at night ensures that he or she will have a rotten night's sleep, and reduces his or her chances of finding a friend for moral support. Breaking up over a breakfast sandwich is smarter than ditching someone over a midnight snack.

- NEVER let a breakup reach the public eyes and ears before you tell the other person. This means no IM's, MySpace™ or Facebook™ posts, or blogging about it. Have respect for the other person regardless of what has taken place in the relationship.

- Having to be somewhere directly afterwards can provide you with a valid and honest exit after the breakup. Limit the meeting to no more than one hour.

- Be kind. There is no reason to pour salt in the wound. If you were hurt by something that happened, then write the person who hurt you a letter and mail it to them... without a stamp. It is ok for you to get it off your chest but not to dump it on someone else. If you want to actually mail the letter, wait 48 hours after writing it and let someone you trust read it before it goes into the mailbox.

- Always remember the Golden Rule: Do unto others only as you would have done unto you. If you think it would be unbearably lame if Jimmy text messaged you at 10:00 pm: "Yo — no go prom. Taking Chelsea instead. Cya," then don't do it to him.

- Above all, be fair. Remember— every relationship involves two people, not just one. A failed relationship is like a fender bender — it is painful and damaging, but you will drive again. What you are trying to avoid are the "driving into a tree" and "sending someone over a cliff" disasters.

> **Sometimes the "wow" factor becomes the "ow" factor.**

Okay we're bringin' this on home.

Your child has been tested all along. Since your daughter first brought home her prized valentine from Benny in the 3rd grade exchange: *Buzz Buzz, Bee Mine*, she has been "dating;" she has been trying out new dating choices. In the 6th grade, your son had a paralyzing crush on Inga, the Swedish exchange student; he couldn't eat his dinner or practice his recorder. In her freshman year, your daughter came home from band camp stone in love with a tuba player who only went by the one-word name of "Lips." So, your kids have been driving around, dating around for years now. But you, the parent, are a little smarter now than you were, say, before you picked up this book. You have begun to realize that just like in driving, these kids need some instruction. You would no more hand the keys to your mini-van over to your 13-year-old than you would set them up on a blind prom date. But you might take them for a short, very well supervised spin around a private subdivision driving 15 miles an hour. My husband and I let our kids drive a golf cart around our two acres when they were in middle school. Good thing. Our daughter ran into a bush the size of Manhattan and dented the trampoline. Fortunately, there were no cars or people to harm, so the risk was minimal. We were able to let them both get a feel for this driving business without injuring anyone.

And that's what I've been trying to share with you for 16 chapters. If we teach these kids how to date from the time they show any interest in it, our chances at creating an "intelligent dater" increase. This is how we teach them to drive. We helmet up our little people and send them tooling around the yard in a Fisher Price Jeep. Even at 4 miles an hour, they still need some guidance. "Try to stay out of mommy's rose bushes, Tyler." When they are six, we helmet them up again and put them on a bicycle. "Stay to the side of the road. And watch out for mommy's rose bushes." And when they turn sixteen we put them in a car and let them pilot the most dangerous vehicle they'll likely ever own.

The rules and guidelines of the road are complex and dangerous, so we instruct our students one level at a time. And at each level we have been testing their knowledge and their skill level. The same is true for dating. At every level of this dating game, as parents, as wise old coots with nothing better to do than meddle in the lives of our young people, we have been guiding and steering and testing their dating lives to try to keep them safe. We have to. They no longer wear helmets. It messes up their hair.

In Driver's Ed, there is a final test that determines if you have gained enough knowledge and skill to have earned the keys. For years, for decades the government has been studying how teens learn to drive to adequately develop this final test. Let's apply these same principals to testing our student for their dating readiness.

These test segments have been pulled from the Michigan *"Road Skills Test Study Guide."*

Test segments must always be given in the following order:

1. *Vehicle familiarization and safety inspection.*
   - *Does your student know where all the knobs and dials are? The emergency brake? The hazard lights?*
   - Does your teen really know their date well enough to be alone with him or her? Is this person safe? What will you do if they become verbally forceful?

2. *Basic control skills test.*
   - *Can you maintain a safe speed? Do you signal your intent? Can you navigate your vehicle without constant over-correction?*
   - Can your student demonstrate that they are in control of the relationship and have the skills to be a good date? Does your teen control their emotions?

3. *On-road driving test.*
   - *Do you turn left in front of oncoming traffic? Do you wait until it is your turn to go at the four-way stop?*
   - Can your child put their words into action and make mature decisions at every dating crossroad?

Encroachments: You are penalized each time your vehicle (your student) *touches a boundary. Can you perform a maneuver without crossing over any boundary lines?* Do they have good physical boundaries that they do not cross or even test the limits of?

Driving test: You must demonstrate your ability to drive (date) *safely over a pre-determined route. The route will contain a variety of situations... and you must operate your vehicle* (your student— mind, body, soul, and emotions) *in a safe and responsible manner, obeying all traffic* (dating) *laws.* Has your student logged a variety of hours in diverse locations to demonstrate their ability to cope with change?

The examiner will observe and score you on specific maneuvers as well as on your general driving behavior including collision avoidance and distractions. Is your student aware that their date's parents and friends have been watching every move they make?

Okay, here's the rest, the final analogy. Even if you pass the driving test, even when the instructor hands you your Graduated Driver's License, it doesn't mean you are done being tested. Every single time you get behind the wheel it is a test. Cops are watching you drive. Are you maintaining safe speeds? Did you cut anybody off? Insurance companies are watching. How many tickets have you accumulated? Your parents are keeping an eye on your driving. Is your vehicle littered with pop cans — or worse? Is there a new piece of bumper missing? A lot of people are paying attention to how you drive. And some aren't paying attention at all. Toddlers aren't. That's right — they're playing Tonka trucks at the end of a cul-de-sac oblivious to you in your Kia with your headphones on. That 12-year-old on the banana seat bike? She has no idea that you are behind her. You are being tested constantly because an error in driving can lead to such epic tragedy.

Ah, dating success. Maybe your students have been following all the dating "rules" and "guidelines" from the very start. Let's say your student has found a real gem of a boyfriend or girlfriend. They have logged well over 60 hours of quality (non-idiot box) hours with this student, they are not bored, they are happy. They have introduced this date to you, and the parental units have actually grown quite fond of this new beau. There are no obvious red flags. Vision is good and all the gauges are in the green. You're all done, right? The test is over? Hand them the dating keys and walk away?

Answer this question about driving, and we'll see. You finally gave in and let your daughter drive herself and her two best friends 150 miles away so that they could attend an all-day Christian music festival. Did you worry while they were on the road? She has her license, so you know she can drive. The car has been gassed up and the oil was changed. You love and trust her two friends; they are "good people." They are on their way to an uplifting and wholesome event, and the sun is shining. Why on earth would you worry? Oh, I don't know, because you're the parent? It's in our genetic code. It's on our resume. We are obligated to be concerned — even if we have done all the research and all the testing. Things could happen. Things we cannot test for.

Now, if you have taught your child well, do you worry less? Yes, actually you do. If you had not seen for yourself that she knows how to merge onto the freeway, change her own tire, and drive within safe speeds, you might not sleep as well at night. But you *did* lead her every step of the way, you *did* teach her how to drive through rush hour traffic, how to parallel park, and to please not talk on her cell phone while she's driving. You trust her to make good decisions. You will worry, but she has shown you that she can do it without you.

The equivalent comparisons hold true in dating. Because you have been monitoring, instructing, and guiding every step of the way, you have some level of trust in your student now. When he goes out on that big prom date, it's not the first time he's dated. His first outing is not with some new girl who just transferred in from Tunisia who's only English phrases are "Cutie pie" and "You want me?" No, you have been steering your son down a healthy dating road for years. He has been following the rules, you have met and approved his date and his style, corrected him when he was wrong and praised him when he was right. And NOW, when you hand over the dating keys, and you send him on his prom date with $100 in his pocket (half of which you "donated" because of a deal you made in Chapter 11) you can relax just a little bit. Will you worry? Of course. It is in your Parental Contract to fret. But, you have taught them well. You were there every step of the way encouraging them to follow the dating "laws," reading the dating signs, learning to respect boundaries. And because of that, they will date with more confidence, and you will sleep with something like peace.

Teaching a child how to drive is a huge commitment. It turns the key to the most powerful weapon most of us will ever operate. The most powerful *mechanical* weapon, that is. Teaching a child how to date might just be an even bigger undertaking. What single weapon on this planet can cause more pain or create more elation than a human heart? Handing over the keys to someone's heart is a far more organic experience. Their hearts have been in training for months, years even, to run this race. You have been helping your student develop strategies and skills to maneuver down the dating highway to protect both their own precious hearts and the hearts of those around them.

No, the test, the test*ing*, is not over. But, because you've been deliberately planning and training for this "graduation day" with your student for such a long time, he or she can drive away down the road, date away down the highway, you can stand on your porch and wave, confident that their hearts are strong enough to make this all important journey.

Drive It Home...

DIA-LOG with your student about their test procedures and results:

Review... You will be observed (and tested) on how well you handle all of the following dating maneuvers (straight out of the Driver's Ed manual!):

- *Selecting a safe and legal speed*
- *Ability to brake and come to a complete stop*
- *Keeping both hands on the wheel*
- *Obstructed vision*
- *Maintain controlled direction*
- *Ability to read signs accurately*

- *Communicate a change in direction and your intentions to others*
- *Maintaining a cushion of space around your vehicle and do not crowd others*
- *Check regularly where children may be present*
- *Ability to keep your head up and remain focused*
- *Taking your eyes off the road for long periods of time or causing distractions*
- *Creating hazardous situations*
- *Obeying all signs signals and laws*
- *Scanning ahead to get the "Big Picture"*
- *Make sure you are in the "gear" (clothing) that is appropriate for the direction and speed you are traveling*
- *Leaving enough space for an escape route, should it be necessary*
- *Be aware and alert and realize others may not be*
- *Be careful and increase your following distance at night*
- *Courtesy to others*
- *Recognize you are sharing the road with others*

Road Trip...

Student:

Thoughts about reflection.

My brother has owned, driven, and continues to restore many cars. He collects memorabilia of these prized vehicles. He can tell you everything he liked or didn't like about every one. He knows from experience what he will look for in the next car he chooses. Looking back at the choices you have made in the past (good or bad) is an excellent way to make educated guesses about your future.

My daughter has a silver locked miniature suitcase she calls her "Ex-box." She keeps a collection of notes, dried flowers, photos, and other mementos from young men she has spent time getting to know before they were "official."

A box like this can hold fresh reminders of what your student has looked for in the past, and what they are looking for in the future. The "Ex-box" is not meant to be shared with others, but instead, to be used to reflect and remember what worked and what didn't work in the hours logged with past "dates." How did I handle that one? How often did this one require repair? Would I choose a similar manufacturer next time?

Make time for reflection. Be sure the rusted out Gremlin does not make it to the showroom pedestal.

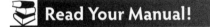 Read Your Manual!

~

"Boys frustrate me. I hate all their indirect messages, I hate game playing. Do you like me or not? Just tell me so I can get over you."

—Kirsten Dunst

"People change and forget to tell each other."

—Lillian Hellman

"The difference between school and life? In school, you're taught a lesson then given a test. In life, you're given a test that teaches you a lesson."

—Tom Bodett

"Don't cry for someone who's left you. The next one may fall for your smile."

—Mae West

"Be who you are and say what you feel because those who mind don't matter, and those who matter don't mind."

—Dr. Seuss

Handing Over the Keys

In the middle of February, we moved from San Diego, California, to Southfield, a suburb north of Detroit, Michigan. What was I thinking? San Diego is where weathermen go to retire. Every day, the same forecast: "Yep, looks like it will be, um, sunny and 76 again today. This is Pete "Shortsleeves" Repeat saying, 'See you tomorrow' when we'll take an in-depth look at T-shirts: Cotton or Poly-blend?" In Detroit, weathermen earn combat pay.

It wasn't just the weather that had changed. My life in California had been a vivid portrait of youthful success. I was twenty-something, blonde, tan, and single. I tossed my psychedelic surfboard into the back of my white Mustang convertible with the red leather seats, and drove six flower-laden blocks to the bright blue ocean. Suddenly, I found myself living in a new state, in a new gray climate, living a white-washed version of my old life. Or should I say beige-washed. I had beige hair, a beige house, a beige dog, a beige husband, two beige kids and worst of all… a beige minivan.

What am I doing with a beige minivan? It's the color of the dust on my tennis racket. I never wanted to be typical or average, let alone colorless. Yet here I was wandering around a parking lot trying to figure out which ugly old-person van was mine, because the entire strip-mall generation seemed to drive these same dreary vehicles. It was hard to let go of my young White Mustang image, but there were reasons so many of my fellow coupon-clippers had opted for the van. It didn't show the dirt like my little red Ford. It got better gas mileage; I could slide a stroller in the back. And the number one reason I traded in White Hot for Background Beige? The side impact rating gave me peace of mind with my precious toddler in tow. It fit me. I was grown up now.

Maybe there are a few of you that married your very first Mustang (figuratively speaking, of course. That's still illegal in most states.) Some of you might actually still be married to your first crush, your first love, your childhood sweetheart. But most of us drove (or dated) a dozen (or more) models before we landed in the driver's seat of our long-term relationship. My relationship with the Army-green Satellite was beaten before it started — rusted out after incurring too much abuse before I ever drove it. The pretty blue Horizon was good and solid, but the constant shifting didn't allow me to talk with my hands (I'm Italian, you know.) The Mazda truck simply came to a cruel, abrupt halt. A shocking, painful end in which it just "stopped." All of us have leased, rented, borrowed, and purchased vehicles suited to a specific moment in our lives. We test-drove many models before we settled for our practical beige vans.

And because we want our kids to succeed us — to outlive us, out-run, out-jump and out-*love* us — we are sharing the hard lessons that we learned during some of the toughest dating years of our lives in order to steer our kids toward healthy, safe, tragedy-free relationships. It's been a long, strange trip, but it's worth it if we can keep our kids off the concrete wall of a dating disaster. Our new motto: "I took the hit so you can keep your teeth."

The moment has come. This is what you've been building up to over the last 16 chapters — handing your kids the dating keys. You picked up this book because you agreed that parents are the best dating guides. Sure, kids could learn about the opposite gender from playground gossip, from lunch line rumors, from band camp hook-ups and MySpace™ chats. But without your ancient wisdom, without the years and thousands of miles of bald tread, all that highway humdrum is just a never ending monotonous whine. It's about as effective as a Matchbox racer in the NASCAR circuit. Bottom line, we want the best for our babies.

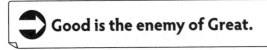 **Good is the enemy of Great.**

Let's look in the rearview mirror. Let's glance back at the road you have traveled with your student.

We agree that dating begins well before "dating" begins. Second graders on the monkey bars are pulling each others' hair as a flirt. Fifth graders who steal kisses under the bleachers are like kids who "pretend drive" daddy's big truck. It starts so early.

Trying to carve a time-line in stone for your child's "first date" is about as useful as carving their shoes out of stone to keep them at home. "You can't date until you're 16" just does not reflect the reality of their daily lives. In their daily locker-leaning, hair-twirling, squealing-over-a-hottie lives, they are dating, or at least practicing dating, long before you have issued them a permit. With or without your guidance, they will ditch their stone shoes and run free.

You have coached them into making good date selections, intelligent choices for logging quality hours. (Elise from soccer, Brandon from band class, somebody with whom they have something in common). They are more perceptive now to recognize those kids whom they should probably NOT invest a lot of time with (Ziggy from prison, anyone named Froot Loop). You have taught them that they are responsible for their choices, and that the car doesn't get the tickets, the driver does.

Kids will, do, and have received dating advice from both reliable and unreliable sources. They have learned how to sift the good from the bad. Just because Erin has been your Best Friend Forever since October, that does not qualify her to give dating advice. She's a lovely girl with pretty hair, but her dating skills were sharpened in the girl's locker room. Uncle Tommy "Shotgun" Foster, with one failed marriage at age 18 that lasted as long as it took for the cake to get stale, and his subsequent, successful marriage that has lasted 23 years, make him a good source of instruction for both what *to* do, and what *not* to do in dating.

You taught your student that in order to even take the Dater's Ed course, they must be qualified. Every student must have ID (who are they — pressed and dressed, or stressed and depressed?), permission (ASK FIRST), and some hard-earned loot (Bank of Dad or Pancake Patty's Paycheck?)

We talked about finding the Perfect One, that every day these kids are out on the showroom floor putting their best strut forward and shining up their grills, doing the Dealership Disco Dance. Everyone is looking at everyone else, making selections and making rejections. You've taught them to look beyond the exterior and look far deeper to the inside at the features that really count — reliability, strength of character, kindness. Analyze the original assembly — did the lug nut fall far from the tree or perhaps out of the tree onto his head?

Together with your student you have assembled a Pit Crew, a group of trustworthy people who have your back (and your side and your rear) who have agreed to keep an eye on your student's dating progress and flag them in for a Pit Stop when they bust a front axle trying to outrun the same elusive redhead lap after lap.

And then, after all the preliminary "classroom work" was complete, it was time to let your student get behind the wheel where the real hand-over-hand driving began. You gave them a key and let them pull away from the curb on their first down-to-the-corner-and-back practice run. Turning that key made sparks fly, but they were small and contained. They didn't set the engine on fire.

We live in a world where Evites have replaced invites, email replaces snail mail, and we text each other with fancy abbreviations on our cell phones instead of talking on them. But even if we agree with our teen that technology is über cool, we have also convinced them that it is no substitute for face-to-face, hand-in-hand dating. You can visit the Caribbean with a click of a button, but a webcam cannot give you a tan and blow sand in your ear.

As their self appointed "Dating Coach," your student is in the driver's seat, and you have agreed to be their co-pilot. You will sit there (with no promise of "quietly") and help them maneuver between the lines and keep their eyes on the road. They have agreed to "date in front of you," to log intentional, quality hours with their potential beaus. They will spend non-idiot-box, non-electronic hours with each other. They will go live and unplugged.

> ➡ **We no longer go next door to borrow a cup of sugar, we just order it online.**

It is only by spending live doing-something-together hours that students can read body language, tone of voice, and facial expressions. Kids must get up off their pockets and move around each other, talk to each other, play games, throw a Frisbee, make a cheesecake. They have to drive, not ride. Only then can they begin to read the signs that describe the journey they're on. As the highly interested parent, you are the interpreter of the difficult signs, the ones obscured by relationship fog or veiled behind an attractive façade of beauty that hides a secret thorn. Or tire-piercing nail that will render them helpless.

You've given your student the supplies to draw indelible boundaries around themselves and instilled in them the self-esteem to defend their perimeters. DO NOT PASS means exactly that. Here is the line, it is drawn in waterproof, smudge-proof, tear-proof paint, and it means, simply, that you, my darling new friend with the wandering hands, need to have a different kind of license to get beyond my tan lines.

As the primary observer, you reserve the right at any time to require your student to pull over and examine his vehicle, his AAA triptych, his MapQuest™. Kick the tires, look under the hood. Once the student has invested a few hours with this particular passenger, analyze whether the ride been smooth. Have they hit the same pothole every time they take that one turn around the "don't go there" block? How many screws are loose?

Your student also understands by now the dire consequences of dating under the influence. It is as dangerous to date under the murky haze of drugs and alcohol as it is to drive that way. If you drive stoned, you might hit a tree. If you date stoned, you hit The Wall of Despair.

You have made known to your child the very real existence of dating hazards and emergencies. Teens have unknowingly "invited" dangerous people into their lives just by going on line and being careless about telling the world their personal data. And as hard as it is to think about this, parents, we must acknowledge that even if we have raised the most sober, well-adjusted, and intelligent teen this side of the Windows–Mac Divide, this does not guarantee that they will not come into contact with drunken, psychotic nut cases who were raised by wolves. There are unthinkable hazards out there, and so we keep track of our precious babies, we demand to know where they are at all times, we look at their MySpace™ pages, and we drop into their rooms unannounced. It may make us unpopular, but if it keeps my baby's face in its current condition of undamaged freshness, do I care?

Then we gave our students a vision test. Cover your left eye and read these letters: O-P-E-N-Y-O-U-R-E-Y-E-S. Use that great brain of yours to absorb the light shooting at you from the past, present, even future. Look back, look around, and train your telescopic pupils to focus on your own goals and dreams. Do not get blinded by the moonlight.

And finally we reminded our students that even if they pass the initial test, even if they are issued a Graduated Dater's License, the testing is never really over. Every day is a test. Every day the cops point their radar at you, the insurance companies aim their statistical tables at your wallet, and well-meaning friends and family are on the sidelines with a cattle prod and a megaphone shouting "I-told-you-so" whenever you make a wrong turn.

Your kid, yes *yours*, is growing up faster than the speed of "Send." In the time it took you to read this book, your child has mastered three new ways to get into trouble. They "level up" to the next dangerous thing at an alarming rate. They are also the most charming, engaging, brilliant, and sensitive souls that God could entrust to our care. Is there anyone you would rather spend time with than your teen? Okay, maybe not every hour of every day, but are they not a constant source of surprise and pride? And who is more creative than a teen? Who else would build a ladder out of a discarded basketball pole then clean your gutters while they were on the roof? Yes you may want to wring their neck with one hand, hug them with the other, and with your third hand sweep up all the clutter in their wake, but what a gift. (Doesn't every parent have three hands?)

They have already learned some important lessons — that people don't care how much you know until they know how much you care. It is hopefully sinking in that they should spend far less time trying to impress people, especially to get a date. You don't walk into a dealership and convince the car that it should go home with you. "Hi, I am in Honors English, I play soccer for the best travel team in the state, and I am on the Homecoming Court. Mind if I drive you home?"

> **Never allow someone to be your priority while allowing yourself to be their option.**

All along you've been teaching your student that learning to build a healthy relationship should start right from the green flag. No, you're not trying to "marry them off," but knowing how to take smart, short trips before they commit to the life-long marriage journey is vital to their future success. In marriage you say "I do" not "I did." It means that you build from each step, each block, each detour to make that relationship work. If you can't get to the corner store, how are you going to get to Neiman Marcus?

Media has tried to convince our kids that every kiss is accompanied by a full orchestra. The reality is that most kisses are accompanied by empty pizza boxes and the sound of flies. That does not diminish the importance of every kiss, every held hand, and every ride through the Tunnel of Love (even if it smells like carp and bleach). It means that our kids should not be swayed by the glossy brochures. Those are just slick marketing campaigns that advertise shine not flaws, blond models not assembly line workers.

And so, you've handed them the keys to date. Issuing them their "Graduated Dater's License" is a gesture of trust and approval that says, "All right, I'm getting out of this car now. I'm still watching, and I can put you on recall at anytime, but go ahead, have fun, enjoy the ride. Call me if you need anything. Here's five bucks for gas." And as they back out of the driveway, wave, and try not to cry. Of course, they'll be back. The title is in your name.